Saying Goodbye Your Way

Planning or Buying a Funeral or Cremation for Yourself or Someone You Love

John F. Llewellyn

Tropico Press®
Glendale, California

Printed in the United States of America

Publisher's Cataloging-in-Publication
(Provided by Quality Books, Inc.)

Llewellyn, John F.
    Saying goodbye your way / John F. Llewellyn
    p. cm
    Includes bibliographic references and index
    LCCN 2002093824
    ISBN 0-9665801-4-1

    1. Funeral rites and ceremonies--United States--
Planning. 2. Death--Social aspects--United States.
I. Title

GT3203.L54 2003   393'.9
                         QBI03-200023

Carol, thanks.

Contents

Figures

Foreword

In cultures more rooted in wisdom than our own, two things have long been understood: (1) that acknowledging our mortality can actually inspire us to live happier, more meaningful lives, and (2) that participating in ceremonies which commemorate the significant transitions in our lives can have a profound healing effect.

Unfortunately, as our culture has become increasingly influenced by technology, we have also become obsessed with clean, quick solutions to our "problems." We are inclined to take short-cuts in matters which, if more consciously attended to, would enhance our experience and understanding of what it means to be alive.

In this wonderful book, John Llewellyn has taken a lifetime of experience and crafted it into a beautiful, comprehensive roadmap designed to guide us through two of life's most significant events— creating and planning funerals for ourselves and creating and planning funerals for our loved ones.

Ceremonies commemorating our own lives and the lives of those we love are important opportunities for the individual, the family, and the community. They are opportunities to heal, to grow, and to be reminded in a meaningful way about the things that really matter in life—love, kindness, generosity, and connection to each other.

This beautiful guidebook will take much of the mystery and fear out of the planning process. It will help us learn to grow through all of life's inevitable transitions. This book should have a place of honor and importance in the library of every home in America. It should be required reading for every member of the family.

And for those who think reading such a book would be depressing, let me just say that hiding our heads in the sand is much more often the cause of depression. Cultivating the ability to look squarely and honestly at the truths of life can be both enlivening and liberating.

In pre-planning a funeral, a family has the opportunity to gather together to face the inevitable reality that sooner or later one or more members of the clan will—at least physically—be gone. It is this recognition, perhaps more than any other, which can inspire us to live our lives fully—to Love each other completely—and to appreciate the preciousness of every day and every moment we have together.

When the inevitable parting takes place, we have the opportunity to give ourselves, our families, and our communities the gift of remembrance and honor; gathering together to love one another, to honor a unique and precious life, and to give each other support in the midst of our grief.

A funeral is a time of love, celebration, remembrance, and transition. We honor a beloved life. We express our gratitude for all that person has given us. We honor the ways in which that special individual has helped us to grow in the experience of love. We honor our sadness about the loss.

And as we say good-bye to our loved ones' earthly forms, we begin the process of transitioning to a new relationship with them. We begin to find the true dwelling place of love—a sacred realm in our own hearts. And, in the process of connecting with our own hearts, we ultimately come to understand that love never dies.

Let each funeral ceremony be a healing bridge to that sacred realm in your own heart—that sacred place of eternal love and connection where true relationships always exists. In that pursuit I offer you a blessing that your life may be enlivened by each inevitable experience of loss: May you come to know that which never changes and never dies—the ocean of love in your own heart.

John E. Welshons
Author of *Awakening from Grief:
Finding the Way Back to Joy*

Preface

Throughout the ages, we've celebrated milestones of life—birth, coming of age, marriage, and death. Ceremonies have developed to observe each of these happenings. Death has been feared, celebrated, worshiped, condemned, and praised. In short, the reactions to it have covered a wide range of human emotions. Despite death being inevitable, most people have not wanted to talk about the end of life.

In some cultures, there existed a fear that talking about death would hasten one's own demise. Even when that cultural bias didn't exist, many avoided speaking of death because it reminded them of their own mortality.

As the baby boomers age, they also are becoming the "sandwich generation," faced with the responsibilities of taking care of both parents and children. With this view of life and death, the boomers are becoming more interested in discussing how to deal with the end of life.

After some thirty-plus years in the cemetery and funeral professions, I've a deep appreciation for family dynamics. I've seen a widow's angst over "not knowing what George would have wanted." I've also seen the relief of families because "Mom and Dad took care of everything ahead of time." As I've mulled over these experiences, I've realized that the biggest value is in having the discussions—and putting something in writing. It's that process that gives the most peace of mind.

This book was written specifically because attitudes about death and the rites that accompany death are changing. Some still perceive a "funeral" as being a rigid ceremony that does not allow a personal approach to acknowledge a person's life in a way that has meaning for family and friends. That doesn't have to be so. It's my hope that through this book people will better understand the options available to them and how they can do it "their way."

I've tried to use terminology that will be familiar to most consumers. Sometimes this isn't precise, but a glossary is included that defines terms related to cemeteries and mortuaries. While I've tried to avoid being repetitious, realizing that some readers will use this book for reference, some duplication of material was necessary.

It's becoming increasingly common for people to pay for their funerals in advance—to prearrange. There are many different ways to pay for a funeral ahead of time. Understanding how each of these methods works can help you make better decisions about whether it makes sense for you to prearrange a funeral or cremation. The material in this book should help you ask the right questions as you develop your own ceremonies to Celebrate A Life®—for yourself or someone you love.

While there are many books about funerals, many have been written by people who do not trust mortuaries. Their solutions often have been to avoid funerals and mortuaries. For many, the services provided by a mortuary have great value when faced with the loss of someone you love. Understanding options and the process should give you confidence to manage the way you say goodbye. A mortuary should be viewed as a resource that can help you get the ceremony you want rather than an institution that will try to push you into something that is not meaningful for you. Hence, the goal of this book is to empower you to be able to have a funeral or cremation the way you want it—whether you are planning your own funeral or a funeral for someone else.

I am indebted to a great many people who over the years have given me an appreciation of the importance of life, living, and planning. I am particularly proud of my association with Forest Lawn Memorial-Parks & Mortuaries. With almost 100 years of experience, Forest Lawn has served hundreds of thousands of families. Forest Lawn has long been known as a leader in the field. In 1917, it launched the memorial-park plan that eliminated tombstones to give way to sweeping vistas of lawn. In 1933, Forest Lawn opened the first mortuary on dedicated cemetery grounds. Having grown from being a small country cemetery in 1906 to having five locations today, Forest Lawn is known for its beauty and outstanding art collection. It's a unique institution in many ways, but the most notable is the quality and caring spirit of those who work there. Day in and day out, they demonstrate not only their commitment to high levels of service, but also their respect and reverence for the thousands of families who have entrusted people they have loved to us—not just for the short time leading up to a funeral service, cremation, or burial, but for eons to come.

Numerous people have given me support during the creation of this book. I would particularly like to thank Anita Wallace for her early help with organization and her valuable suggestions about grieving. Carol Caunter provided a wonderful perspective of how to make the text more consumer-friendly. From her years of involvement with prearrangement, Nancy Kremin's insights helped me focus and refine my message. Bob Fells' comments helped to smooth out some rough spots and make the text more universal than my California perspective. Lee Lewis' editing skills helped refine the final manuscript. A special thank-you goes to my assistant, Kim Pawlik, for her patient review of many drafts. Each of their suggestions helped refine the structure of the book as well as improve the clarity of explanation of some of the concepts. However, I didn't always follow their advice, so whatever problems remain are all mine!

I sincerely hope that this book will help people be more in control when planning for saying goodbye or going through the agony of losing someone close to them. I believe that it is not only possible, but also important, that you be able to say goodbye your way.

Disclaimers

Many things discussed in this book are subject to specific state statutes. Although efforts have been made to use generalities that will apply in most instances, the reader is cautioned always to seek authoritative advice based on the laws in any given specific jurisdiction. The author and publisher do not advocate consumers or businesses breaking the law or not complying with any governmental requirement or regulation. This book is not intended to be professional legal, accounting, medical, or psychological advice. Readers should consult appropriate qualified professionals based upon their own individual situation.

The opinions expressed in this book are those of the author and do not necessarily reflect the opinions, policies, or positions of any organization with which he is affiliated..

Saying Goodbye

Death is nothing at all.
I've only slipped away into the
next room.
I am I and you are you.
Whatever we were to each
other, that we still are....
Life means all that it ever
meant.
It's the same that it ever was....

Henry Scott Holland

1. The Inevitable

Times are changing. At least that's what we're told. However, we're periodically reminded that some things don't change. The sun still rises in the east and sets in the west. The cycle of birth and death is unending. The mortality rate is fixed at one hundred percent per person. Rationally, we know we're mortal, but it sometimes takes the loss of someone close to us to remind us of our own mortality.

Often it seems easier not to talk about the fact that we will, someday, leave life as we know it now. As for what is beyond that, people have their individual beliefs. Some have found the answer in their religion, others have developed their own vision, and some have reconciled themselves to a view that "when it's over, it's over."

No matter what your beliefs, however, sometime during your life you will be confronted by death. It might be from the loss of a family member—a parent, grandparent, spouse, brother, sister, or, tragically, a child—or from the death of a friend, coworker, or even a public figure. Personally, I've attended funerals for my parents, grandparents, aunts, uncles, cousins, friends, and coworkers. But I've also been touched by the deaths of people I never met. Like many, I remember vividly where I was when I learned that John F. Kennedy had been shot. I know where I was when Christa McAuliffe died when the Challenger space shuttle exploded right after takeoff. I remember watching the coverage of Princess Diana's funeral. I can't shake the image of the devastation from the September 11, 2001, attacks on America.

Within my own family, I've seen people struggle with how to talk about death—their own or that of other family members. My grandfather thought that talking about buying a cemetery space would somehow accelerate the end of his life. At the other end of the spectrum, my great uncle, Hubert Eaton, thought a lot about his funeral, and was clear about what he wanted. Interestingly, my father never really talked to me about his funeral, even though we'd worked together at Forest Lawn for several decades. But he did tell my step[-]mom that he wanted a "service just like Dr. Eaton's."

The point, of course, is that too many people are thrust into dealing with death without having seriously thought about what to do. This is true whether it's the death of family members or one's own passing. Therefore, the goal of this book is to help people talk about the subject and to make plans that let them say goodbye the way they want to. It's my hope that by talking about the subject of death that families will become closer and feel more in control as they go through life's passages.

Thus, this book attempts to help you answer questions about how you want to say goodbye your way—whether you are planning for yourself or for someone you love—by discussing what funerals are, who they are for, and why some rite of passage is important. It also is valuable to personalize services so they are meaningful to family and friends. Of course, there are many ways to do this, so there is considerable discussion about the options available. As most people have little experience with the process of making final arrangements, either before death has occurred or when a loss has happened, I've also included material about the practical aspects of planning and buying funerals, cremations, and burials. I believe that consumers who understand their options are more likely to be satisfied with the decisions they make. It's my hope that you will not only be comfortable with your financial decisions, but also will be able to have services that reflect the uniqueness of you or the person you cared about. I want you to be able to say goodbye your way. ✦

2. What Is A Funeral?

In the simplest terms, a funeral is a ceremony that recognizes the death of someone. It's held to honor and remember a life that has passed. For many, it's also a time to reflect upon their faith or philosophy of life. University of Minnesota sociologist Robert Fulton says that a funeral is not only a declaration of a death that has occurred, but it's also a testimony to a life that has been lived.

A "traditional" funeral is sometimes perceived as being primarily a religious service governed by religious dogma. Although this perception lingers, most funerals have become more personal, reflecting the life of the deceased. Many funerals are no longer just a religious ceremony held in a specific place with a prescribed content. Families have found that they can have funerals that are a combination of religious observance and recognition of an individual. Now, families and friends seek ways to meet their need to remember the unique human qualities of someone they have lost in a way that is meaningful to them while respecting whatever religious beliefs they may have.

Increasingly, society has clamored for a more personal approach from all businesses. Funerals have been subject to the same pressure as society in general. People have come to expect that they can plan and have a funeral the way they want it. The words they use to describe their desires might be "simple" or "I don't want a fuss over me." Some of this may stem from a distrust of organized religion, a desire to have a unique experience (the "boomer" way), or concern that a mortuary might pressure them or their family to overspend on a service or casket. For others, this desire may simply be a need to put things "in order" or to be in control.

I can remember one of the first funerals I attended, shortly after I had gone to work for Forest Lawn. It was for an executive who had been my boss when I worked at Forest Lawn during a couple of summer vacations while I was in college. George was a big tall guy with a gentle sense of humor who was loved and respected by everyone who worked with him. He was full of life and had a wonderful, warm personality. What struck me about his service was that it could have been about anyone. George just happened to be the one who died and triggered it. Little was said about George other than his name was put in a program and he got a small mention during the service.

As I remember it, there were scripture readings, the officiate talked about a Bible passage, and there was a soloist. I came away feeling disappointed. Somehow George had gotten lost in the process. The service didn't help me come to grips with losing someone whom I considered a friend and mentor, and the funeral ritual didn't seem to adequately mark the passing of someone who was so vibrant that several hundred people turned out for his service. Moreover, the content of the service was dictated by the religious denomination.

Looking back, I now realize that the service didn't help

me say goodbye to this man who had been kind to me and whom I respected.

This recitation is not meant to be a criticism of any religion. Every denomination has the right to set its own practices and standards. However, that doesn't mean that each person doesn't have the freedom to practice religion as they desire.

I can't help but contrast George's service with another one I attended more than twenty-five years later. This was a funeral for another longtime Forest Lawn employee, Ann—or Annie as we called her. The service was held in a church of the same denomination, but it had a very different feel. Several people spoke in addition to the pastor. They talked about her quirks and endearing qualities. Those attending shared a chuckle as they remembered this wonderful woman and her eccentricities. While much of the same religious content was there, the service was about Annie. I came away feeling that those attending had shared memories and had said an appropriate goodbye to our friend.

The "Simple" Service

When asked about funerals, consumers in focus groups often talk about wanting a "simple service." While some who use the term do indeed mean "no frills," others mean that they don't want to be forced into someone else's structure.

In some cases, this is a rebellion against their perception of the inflexibility of organized religion. It's somewhat ironic, though, that many who express this point of view don't realize that many religious denominations now recognize a funeral as a complex event that meets a number of needs.

In other cases, it's just a desire for individuality. Often, our counselors—the people who help families with final arrangements—find that families who say they want a "simple" service end up with a service that is anything but simple. That's fine because the label shouldn't be important. The crucial thing, and the reason for this book, is to help people get the type of service they want—to help them think about what they want in a service, to understand some of the options available, and to feel free to express their own individual desires and beliefs.

At Forest Lawn, we often find that what many families really want is an individualized, personalized service rather than a "simple" service—they just don't know how to express that desire or know how many options they have.

"Traditional" Funeral Services

A traditional funeral service is usually held in a church or chapel. This could be the church attended by the deceased or the family or a chapel on the premises of the mortuary or cemetery. At a traditional service, the deceased is present and the casket may be open or closed. (Some religious denominations do not allow an open casket.)

Traditional services usually are conducted by a member of the clergy, and eulogies may be given by friends or family members. Often there is music and sometimes there will be a soloist. The clergyperson generally will read some scripture and will deliver a brief message.

In most cases, at the conclusion of the service in the church or chapel, there will be a funeral procession to the burial site for a brief committal service.

Graveside Service

A graveside service is held at the burial space. It applies to all kinds of cemetery property: burial in the ground, entombment in a mausoleum crypt, or placing cremated remains in a niche in a columbarium. Unlike a committal service, a graveside service is not part of a service held someplace else, like a church. Generally, a graveside service is rather short, but not as short as the committal service that follows a traditional funeral.

Memorial Service

A memorial service honors the deceased without the deceased being present. However, the content of a memorial service is often similar to what would have been included if the deceased were there.

Why have a memorial service? One of the most common reasons is that the burial will take place in another town or that the actual committal service will only be for family members. A memorial service is frequently viewed as a good way to have a second service that allows more people to attend. Some families choose memorial services because they believe that it's morbid to have the deceased there. However, there are some good psychological reasons for having the casket present, whether or not it's open.

The Weight of Traditions

I am a great believer in the philosophy that there is little that is really black or white—especially when it comes to funerals. Mostly, there is no right or wrong, so let me give you some thoughts about the pro[s] and cons of doing things the "traditional" way.

Many families have traditions that they follow on holidays—turkey at Thanksgiving, roast beef on Christmas Eve, and so on. The family gains comfort, togetherness, and a sense of continuity from following these traditions. One of the greatest reasons for having a traditional service is the comfort of a familiar ritual—there is a certain peace and reassurance that comes from doing it the way Grandpa did it.

Traditional funeral services can seem easier to arrange because there is already an established pattern. Sure, there are decisions to be made, but it may seem like less effort than building your own service from scratch. In any case, the traditional funeral service is really only a framework. Having a traditional funeral service should not prevent you from personalizing it in a way that makes it meaningful for you, your family, and friends.

Why Have Funerals?

One of the things that distinguishes human beings from other animals is our capacity to feel, to have emotions. Although no two people experience anything in exactly the same way, many emotions are common to human experience regardless of time in history, place in the world, or culture. The most obvious of these emotions are love, hate, joy, and fear. As a result, people have an ability to bond with other people in a way that transcends simple biological perpetuation of the species. In addition to pairing off, we form relationships that are based upon common experiences, respect, and friendship. Similarly, we recognize the commonality of emotions in many ways including art, literature, and music.

It's because of the richness and breadth of these interactions with other people that every society has developed rites of passage to celebrate and observe major life transitions, including birth, coming of age, graduations, marriage, and death. The rite of passage that acknowledges the death of someone close to us generally has been part of some kind of ceremony known as a funeral.

For many, a funeral is an important religious rite and a time for reaffirmation of faith. It also is the recognition that a life has ended—someone who was a friend, lover, or colleague is no longer with us. Death has physically separated us.

Funerals have been a part of the social and spiritual fabric of society for thousands of years and have always been important events where people have honored life, shared grief, and showed their support for those left behind. In some cultures, the funeral is a vital step in religious rituals that send the deceased into the afterlife.

While there are critics of the funeral profession who try to say that funerals are unnecessary, independent research has repeatedly confirmed the value of a funeral as a sound beginning of the grieving process and an important recognition of a loss.

Who Are Funerals For?

A funeral is mostly for those left behind. At the time of a death, the family is just beginning to realize its loss and a funeral is a way to put the loss into perspective. Funerals that honor the life of the deceased are a way for family and friends to acknowledge the fact that a death has occurred. Additionally, the funeral is a time to recognize the enormity of the situation as well as the personal loss of a special person with unique attributes, quirks, and idiosyncrasies. It's a time for people to connect—to share feelings and memories. By reflecting on the life of one who has left us, we find time to renew our beliefs, our faith, and our spiritual values.

Dr. Therese Rando, noted psychologist and author, states, "Funerals assist you in beginning to accommodate the changed relationship between yourself and your deceased loved one."[1] As a rite of passage, funerals play an important role in helping us assimilate life transitions. Many kinds of funerals can fulfill this need, but it's hard to skip the transitional step of a funeral itself. For many, the formal recognition of the death of another through some sort of ceremony is an important step in the grief process.

Throughout time, funerals have varied enormously. State funerals of monarchs and political heroes have often marked not just the passing of an individual but also a transfer of power. Funerals of celebrities have often drawn many admirers who want to acknowledge their tie to someone they have never met, but who touched their lives in some significant way. So, in some instances, funerals are for far more people than those who actually attend the service.

Funerals are a time for expressing personal beliefs. For the person who has died as well as those left behind, the faith-value of the service depends upon one's religious beliefs. Some religions call for a service that has a very precise order and set of rituals, while others will only have more generalized guidance. Either way, most religions hold that ritual recognition of death is important.

Most discussions of funerals focus on the deceased and those who attend the service. However, when you think about what you want in the event of your own death, it may have an emotional impact on you and those who are close to you. For most who do this, it isn't just a practical act of planning for their own death; it's a priceless act of love and caring. When you plan your own funeral, you think about your life, what is important to you, and the relationships you've had. In fact, the process often brings a sense of tranquility, peace of mind, and comfort and often can have the effect of bringing people closer together.

A Funeral Is...

If you ignore labels, a funeral can be designed just about any way you want. It can be very structured and follow the dictates of your religion or can be entirely free-form. To me, the goal of a successful funeral is to focus on the person rather than activities, like burial.

You shouldn't feel locked-in, limited, or put off by the term "funeral." In fact, perhaps a more general term should be used, as funerals may be almost anything a family wants. The term "celebration" is offensive to some cultures, for they feel it's disrespectful to "celebrate" a death. So, in an effort to use a non-limiting, non-offensive term, for the balance of this book I'll generally use the term "Ceremony" to mean any sort of service that related to someone's death.

A ceremony is a complex blend of the personality of the deceased with the needs of family and friends. It's neither wrong to spend money or not to spend money, but it is important to think about everyone's needs. However, doing what is "right" in the eyes of others can be very wrong. The death of someone you care about is a time for family and friends to bond, share, and come closer together. Denying your emotional needs is a mistake. Listen to your heart. If traditional rituals give your family comfort and help with the process of grieving, that is okay. But if your family doesn't want to feel bound to the "old way" and wants to invent its own personalized service, that also is okay. The goal is to have a meaningful emotional experience—in other words, to "say goodbye your way." ✻

3. It's Personal

No two people experience another person in exactly the same way. Each relationship we have with others is unique. Although we might share some common experiences with another person, each interrelationship is different. For example, while many parents strive to treat their children equally, in an absolute sense, it's impossible. Relationships other than parent-child have even more variables, because it's unusual, if not impossible, for different people to experience interactions with others in the same way. Each of us has an idea of what "love" is, but each of us also experiences it differently. Each person is unique, and the product of interaction between any two people is also unique. So it naturally follows that any sort of Ceremony to observe the passing of someone close to you is a very personal experience.

The most meaningful and successful Ceremonies recognize the individuality of the person who is gone, addressing the common and shared interactions and experiences with the person as well as honoring their unique attributes. Therefore, when planning a Ceremony, whether for yourself or someone you love, it's important to have some idea of the tone of the Ceremony you think would be most meaningful.

The Rules

In the past, dealing with death was something that only happened when death actually occurred. The funeral ritual was rather rigid—often dictated by one's religious affiliation and heavily influenced by local custom.

As times have changed and the subject of grief has been studied extensively, families have been given access to more information about the process of dealing with death as well as about providers and prices. With more and more flexibility allowed by organized religions, the Ceremony is no longer just a prescribed, formal, impersonal ritual. Progressive mortuaries have recognized that a one-size-fits-all approach just doesn't meet consumers' needs or desires. In short, people can now say goodbye the way they want to.

For the most part, there are no rules when it comes to a Ceremony. Although "appropriateness" is always a fair question, today the answers to the question are rooted much more in the character of the deceased and the individualism of the family than in community expectations. Families now have more control over Ceremony decisions than ever before.

However, even though families have a great amount of flexibility, I don't want to give the impression that families might not find some obstacles to really off-the-wall ideas. Some members of the clergy have limits concerning the content of services they are willing to participate in. These limits may be a result of their denomination's theology or based upon their personal

beliefs. Similarly, funeral directors may be unwilling to participate in a service that they feel is "over the line" of acceptable
community practice.

At Forest Lawn, we've sometimes been asked to do unusual things. One man wanted to put a favorite fishing rod in
the casket with his father (no problem). People have wanted
to be buried with their pets (can't do it—it's against California
state law to bury pets in a cemetery for people[1]). The relatives
of a banking executive really wanted the CEO of the bank to
attend the Ceremony, so they asked us to allow the CEO's
helicopter to land near our church (since the family wanted
this, we did allow the chopper to land). Examples of different
situations could go on and on.

Celebrate A Life®

Increasingly, people seem to want a Ceremony to celebrate
and honor the life of the person who has just died. Grief and
sorrow often are still part of the experience, but these Ceremonies are recognition of the joy of having known a unique individual. There is a desire to recognize that uniqueness—the
good, the not so good, and the humorous. The intent is to be
respectful, but upbeat.

The result of this shift in focus is a much more individualized
Ceremony. Generally, life celebrations elicit a very broad range
of emotions—not just feelings of loss, but also warm memories,
laughter, and a sense of family and community. Of course, there is
some sadness when we have to say goodbye to someone we love.
However, most of us also value the good times, the foibles, and
the quirks. Ceremonies that celebrate a life deal with the entire

life. This is a change from older views of Ceremonies where only the end of life was dealt with, creating somber, sad events.

It's About Dad

A generation ago, making funeral arrangements was often about "burying Dad." That view has shifted to a more positive emphasis on the service being "about Dad." Increasingly, we hear people talk about Ceremonies in terms of their need to remember and honor someone as well as wanting to recognize the deceased's human qualities and uniqueness. You may well have heard someone talking about their own Ceremony saying, "I don't want a service; I want a big party!" That captures the spirit of a life celebration. People celebrate the lives of people they love and honor by having highly personal, emotionally meaningful services. But "emotional" doesn't just mean an outpouring of grief and sadness. A good life celebration usually includes laughter, tears, and warm memories—the emotions that make up the rich fabric of life and are an indication that we've truly bonded with others.

The personalized nature of celebrations of life make them all the more difficult to explain. Often, there will be pictures of favorite activities or family outings. Sometimes there are objects that represent the life being remembered. Here are some examples:

> John was a golfer. He treasured his Saturday morning games with his buddies. Because this was such an important part of his personality and life, his family brought his golf clubs and golf shoes to his memorial service. He had this old, battered golf hat that they gave a place of special prominence. They remembered him that way and knew that he would want to be remembered in the

same light. His golf buddies told some of their favorite golfing stories as part of the service.

Because she was an avid reader, Sally belonged to a book club. At each of the monthly meetings a few of the members of her book club would report on a book they had read. They'd talk about their favorite passages and what they liked, or didn't like, about a book. The members of her book club put together a collage of the covers of Sally's favorite books for her service. Then they had a few laughs about the things she never liked that authors did and shed a few tears about what a romantic she was.

Bobby had been a trucker for most of his life. He'd driven big rigs all over the western United States. In the course of his career, he'd made countless friends on the road. It seemed especially fitting that his final drive was made up of a fleet of big rigs driven by his road buddies.

Alice was an avid hiker. She loved the local mountains and would spend most Saturdays trekking the trails with friends. Her friends and family just couldn't see having a memorial service for her in a church, so after having a small, private burial in a local cemetery, they had a memorial service for her on one of her favorite trails. They personalized it by taking her walking stick and favorite floppy hiking hat. They told stories of blisters, snakes, lizards, and the rainstorm that caught her by surprise. They remembered Alice and what a character she was. They celebrated her life.

The trend is to have Ceremonies that reflect the complexity of life and relationships, celebrate the ups and downs of life, cherish memories, and recognize the uniqueness of each individual. Many have found that they are fulfilled by a Ceremony that is "about Dad" rather than about death.

Having It Your Way

Prearranging a Ceremony is a way to make sure that your family knows what you want. In fact, in California, if you plan your Ceremony ahead of time and provide a way to pay for it so there is no cost to your survivors, your wishes must be followed. There is more on prearranging in later chapters. However, sometimes there is a conflict between the wishes of the deceased and the desires of the family. Some families have coped with this by deciding to have two services, one that follows the wishes of the deceased and another that follows the wishes of the remaining family members.

For example, Andrea's mother was very clear that she wanted only a graveside Ceremony and for only the immediate family to be present. The family honored her wishes, but a week later had a big "fun and sad memorial service" to celebrate her mother's life. With a little creativity, it's possible to accommodate a variety of desires.

As more people are discussing Ceremonies with their families, many are finding they want to consider the feelings and needs of family members as well as having a Ceremony that meets their own needs and beliefs.

Most mortuaries are willing to be quite flexible about the structure and content of Ceremonies. They not only want to allow you to have a Ceremony your way, they want to help you say goodbye in a way that is meaningful for you and your family. ✸

4. Grief & Mourning

Grief is a universal human emotion. It comes with many of life's losses, not just the death of someone you love. While grief may be something that has universality, at the same time it is a unique emotion that everyone experiences differently. This is similar to the concept of love. Everyone "knows" what love is, but once you go beyond the superficial descriptions, it's unique to individuals and individual relationships.

It is important to recognize that the emotion of grief is part of being human. Experiencing grief isn't a sign of weakness or frailty—it is part of who we are as human beings. Identifying the feeling of grief is recognition of an emotional reaction to a loss. That recognition is a healthy and important step toward putting the loss into perspective as we only feel grief as a result of an emotional attachment to someone. The emotion of grief, of course, isn't confined to the death of someone we love. Other life events also can cause grief—divorce, job loss, or the loss of other things we hold dear.

As grief has been studied, it has been found that even though each person experiences grief differently, there are some common emotional and physical reactions to the loss of someone you love. The recognition of the commonality of these responses has given many people comfort. Knowing that others have had similar reactions often helps to understand the journey through grief.

Emotional Reactions

Numbness, Shock, Denial—Often a first reaction is, "This must be happening to someone else, this can't be happening to me." The process of arranging a funeral service often helps overcome denial, as denial stands in the way of allowing the process of grieving to take its normal course.

Anger—"Why did God (fate) do this?" At this stage, it's common to blame friends or other people. You might even be angry with the person who died—Why didn't they take better care of themselves, stop smoking, or exercise more? The feelings of anger or rage also can be accompanied by aggression or irrational resentment.

Guilt—Feeling that you didn't do enough for the person who died. You should have called another doctor, spent more time with them, or been "nicer." Sometimes you may feel guilty that you feel "okay" again, but have the conflicting emotion that you shouldn't ever feel good again.

Panic—You may feel as if you are losing your mind or that something is seriously wrong with you. You may want to run away or disappear. You may have thoughts of harming yourself.

Relief—If there was a prolonged illness, you may feel relief that the person you were close to is no longer suffering. Or perhaps you may feel relief that you are no longer responsible for taking care of them.

Moodiness—You may cry unexpectedly, or whenever someone offers you kind words or comfort. You may get angry unexpectedly and lash out at people.

Secondary Losses—You may find it unexpectedly difficult or emotional to do tasks once performed by the person who died. For example, if they always balanced the checkbook, you might be angry with them for leaving you with that task, and you might find it difficult to do yourself.

Physical Reactions

Sleep Disturbance—Your sleep patterns may change. You may dream often of the person who died, and this may be either comforting or disturbing to you. If your spouse died in the bed you shared, it may be uncomfortable for you to sleep in that bed, or you may fear sleeping alone.

Appetite Disturbance—You may not feel like eating; food may taste like sand or have no taste at all. You may also eat too much. You may feel nauseated or have an empty hollow feeling in your stomach.

Reminders—You may have a need to keep something with you that belonged to the person who died, or you may want to be around their things. The opposite reaction is also common. For instance, you may want someone else to clean out the closet. In this, it's important to remember that you may feel differently some day. If you ask someone to remove all of the deceased's belongings, ask them to keep them for you somewhere until you are sure that you don't want any of them returned to you.

Other Symptoms—You may have other symptoms such as tightness in your chest, you may need to sigh more often than usual, and everything may seem leaden or heavy.

Each of these reactions may come and go, or you might not experience some of them at all. Grief isn't a process that goes from point A to point B to point C. Grieving individuals will typically feel many of these emotions as well as experiencing some of the physical reactions. However, there is no particular order or length of time for these feelings and reactions. Just because you experience one of the emotional responses one day doesn't mean you're through with it and won't experience it again at another time.

Also, grief doesn't happen just because a loss has occurred. It also can be triggered by anticipation of a loss. The anticipation or projection of the feelings we will have when we lose someone close to us can cause deep feelings of grief. Many people begin to experience grief when they are told that someone close to them is terminally ill. Recognizing this is important, because that recognition can help us to understand and react to the emotions being felt.

Talk About It

Many people want to avoid talking about death because it makes them uncomfortable. Generally, the older people get, the more comfortable they are with discussing end-of-life issues.

Not only do younger people tend to be more uncomfortable discussing the subject of death, they sometimes are unwilling to listen when their parents or grandparents do want and need to talk about it. A response of "Oh, Mom, you're not going to die" and then trying to change the subject isn't helpful. Seniors need to talk about issues related to death, and they can feel very lonely when no one will listen to them.

Talking about views of life and death, values, and beliefs can be very helpful in dealing with grief and in planning to say goodbye. The discussions can be beneficial to everyone. Family members can grow closer through these discussions and also can get a better understanding of the desires of the other members of the family. Some of the things people talk about are how they want to die (death with dignity), spirituality, and fears of the end of life as well as how they want to be remembered. During these conversations it's important to be sensitive and compassionate—these types of discussions cannot be forced; people have to be ready.

Goodbye Your Way

I am standing on the seashore.

A ship spreads her white sails to the morning breeze and starts for the ocean. I stand watching her until she fades on the horizon, and someone at my side says, "She is gone."

Gone where? The loss of sight is in me, not in her. Just at the moment when someone says, "She is gone," there are others who are watching her coming. Other voices take up the glad shout, "Here she comes," and that is dying.

Henry van Dyke

5. Ceremonies

A Ceremony should be personalized, so there isn't a clear "right" way or "wrong" way to have one. It should reflect both how the deceased wanted to say goodbye as well as how the friends and family want to say goodbye.

Thus, rather than presenting a set of canned formulas, this chapter discusses some of the possible elements that could be used to personalize Ceremonies. Many of these ideas are equally applicable to developing an individualized Ceremony for prearranging purposes or for a service that is imminent.

Where Should A Ceremony be Held?

Ceremonies can be held in a variety of places, but they are most commonly held in churches or mortuary chapels.

Members of churches often want to hold services for their family members in their own church. The surroundings are familiar and close to members of the congregation. When the deceased or the family is active in a particular church or other place of worship there is a sense of comfort in having the Ceremony in familiar surroundings. However, many churches are quite large. Ten, twenty, or thirty friends and family members may feel lonely in a large church with room for several hundred worshippers. Some members of the clergy and certain denominations strongly encourage this choice—to the extent that some denominations only perform the rituals of their faith in their own facilities.

Many mortuaries have chapels. Although these are often simple nondenominational facilities, the size, quality, and amenities vary a great deal. Family members sometimes like to sit together as a group and prefer to sit separately from their friends during the Ceremony. Some mortuaries make this separation possible by having a "family room" as part of their chapels. If you are considering using a mortuary's chapel, you may want to visit several mortuaries to see exactly what their facilities are like.

It has become more common for cemeteries to have mortuaries on their grounds. As a result, many families have found it more convenient to have the service at the cemetery. This helps avoid a procession through city streets with seemingly inevitable conflicts between the normal flow of traffic and the procession. Another advantage is that the length of the Ceremony isn't extended by the time needed to organize a procession and get it through city streets.

Families who do not wish to have the deceased present often hold memorial services. Although these Ceremonies may be in a church, they also may be in some public place like a park, on top of a mountain, or at the beach. Later in this chapter, there is a discussion about having the deceased present at a Ceremony.

How Long Should It Last?

The length of the Ceremony is determined by how much you're trying to put into it. The general rule followed by most public speakers is that it's better to leave the audience wishing that there were more because it was so interesting rather than having them wish the speaker would finish.

One of the worst Ceremonies I ever went to was for a friend, Bob, who I'd known for a number of years as part of a speaking club. Well, his kids liked to talk, too. Each of them—all three—talked for almost half an hour. What made it so terrible was that not only did each of them say the same thing, the same way, several times, but each of them also told the same stories. While I know they loved their father very much, the way the Ceremony dragged on didn't do him justice and it became agonizing.

I contrast that with another Ceremony I recently attended. Three kids again. In this service, the kids obviously had talked about what each of them would say and coordinated their presentation as to both content and length. There was no overlap, and each of the children covered a distinct part of their father's life. The result was a wonderful, loving presentation about their father. Although I had met their father, I didn't know him well. After the Ceremony was over, I had a real sense of who he was and what was important to him.

There's an old story about a famous professor being approached to give a talk about what was happening in his field. He was asked how long it would take him to prepare the speech. He replied, "If you want me to talk for an hour, I can do it right now. However, if you only want me to talk for five minutes, better give me a week." The moral of this is that short and poignant is usually better than long and rambling, but it does take advance preparation.

Who Should Speak Or Participate?

When trying to determine who should speak or participate in the Ceremony, start by deciding what you want to accomplish—what you want the Ceremony to be like. Here are some questions to ask yourself:

* What part do I want religion to play in the Ceremony?

* Will I, or others who are close to the deceased, get comfort from a familiar ritual?

* Are there close friends who would be able to speak well?

* Is it better to have many people speak or just a few who really know me or my loved one?

The answers to these questions are closely related to other questions about how the Ceremony will be organized. Having too many people speak tends to make a long Ceremony, often pockmarked with redundancies. Also, not everyone is comfortable speaking in public, so that is a factor. I've heard some very moving funeral testimonies from people who aren't accustomed to public speaking, but I've also been at funerals where poor or unprepared speakers made the Ceremony much less poignant.

Not long ago, I attended a Ceremony for a friend of mine who had passed away after a long bout with cancer. He was a very prominent person in the community who was loved and respected by many. His written instructions to his family were that he didn't want a funeral where anyone spoke. He wanted his family to have a big party at his country club and for everyone to just have a good time. Well, some of the local luminaries couldn't resist saying something. So they announced that there would be about fifteen minutes of remarks before the party began. I'm not sure how long the speeches went, but people began to leave after an hour of oration.

If you wish to emphasize spirituality or religious beliefs, a member of the clergy will probably be at the top of your list to officiate at the Ceremony. Conversely, if you're trying to downplay or avoid religion, clergypersons may not even make it on the list of possible speakers.

The choice of who will participate depends upon what you expect of the speakers and their relationship with you or the person you loved. Knowing the tone you want will help you develop a Ceremony that allows you to say goodbye your way.

The Open Mike

With increasing frequency, Ceremonies are being opened up to anyone who wants to speak. Although this is a judgment each family must make for itself, there is some a considerable downside.

First, the people who get up and take the microphone (literally or figuratively) are generally going to be speaking without any preparation or advance thought. In the real world, not too many people do well speaking "off the cuff." Think about politicians that do it—usually they just ramble on and on, and they make their living talking!

Second, an open mike session tends to get redundant very quickly. People haven't had a chance to coordinate what will be said, so the obvious is often repeated.

Third, an open mike increases the chance that someone may get carried away with things that are irrelevant (like talking about themselves rather than the deceased) or inappropriate ("good ol' Joe had a great relationship with his bookie").

Fourth, it's hard to rein it in once people start taking turns. As each additional person gets up to speak, others begin to feel that they should say something, too. This can lead to the foregoing problems as well as extending the time far longer than appropriate.

Is it all bad? Of course not. An open mike as part of a Ceremony can make people feel connected and the opportunity to share can bring richness to a service. One of the most intimate services I remember was for my Aunt Elizabeth. There were only about six people at the graveside service. Each person had a chance to share a memory and we talked about the cycle of life with the family minister who officiated.

Family Member Participation

Many families wonder if a member of the family should participate in the Ceremony. It really depends on the individual. Some family members may be shy about public speaking, even without the stress of the death of someone they are close to, but many times family members are struggling with their own grief to such a degree that they are not able to stand up and speak before a group.

However, being a believer in personalized services, I also must say that there is nothing quite so moving as a family member sharing a warm or amusing experience. Sometimes these shared stories bring back memories of similar occasions. At other times, the stories let a person learn something they didn't know about the person—something that helps them understand the person better.

I believe in emotionally rich services, so I think the idea of having a family member participate is wonderful. On the other hand, no one should be cajoled or coerced into participation if they don't feel they are up to it. Participation can be cathartic and a true act of love, but it also can be way too much pressure on someone in grief.

If family members plan on speaking, discuss what to do if they become overwrought and cannot carry on (or if they get carried away and go on and on). With a contingency plan in mind, any embarrassment or awkwardness should be minimized if a problem does pop up. If the speakers have written out their remarks, a copy can be given to a non-family member who is willing to step in if the speaker cannot carry on.

Casket (Pall) Bearers

These are people chosen by the family to carry or move the casket to the place of burial. These people are generally individuals who were close to the deceased or to the family. Although many refer to "pall bearers," this term is mostly out of date. The origin of the term was from the pall—a piece of cloth—that was placed over the casket. Over time, it has become less common to use palls, although some churches still require their use.

Asking people to be casket bearers or honorary casket bearers is one way to involve people in the Ceremony. For example, at a Ceremony for a longtime Forest Lawn executive, his widow specifically asked that current members of management join the sons in carrying the casket.

When possible, the casket is actually placed on a wheeled cart, so the casket bearers can hold on to the casket and move it on the cart. Often the casket will have to be lifted onto the lowering device at the burial site or carried when conditions prevent the use of a wheeled cart.

Sometimes there are honorary casket bearers who do not actually move the casket but walk immediately behind it. This is a way to include and honor people who are close to the family or to the deceased, but without the physical task of handling the casket.

Humor?

There are those who feel humor is not appropriate for a Ceremony. They feel that it should be a solemn, somber event. After all, someone has died.

On the other hand, humor is part of life. Life is about experiences. Joy and humor are as much a part of the human experience as are sadness and grief. Humor, when used in a loving way, can add depth and warmth to a Ceremony. Most of us would like our friends and families to remember us for the good times, for the shared joy and laughter. Humor can help do that—naturally, not humor that mocks anyone or is cruel or sarcastic, but humor that helps define an individual's uniqueness.

In a previous section, I remarked that many people say they "don't want a funeral" they just want a "big party." Well, what makes a party? Laughter, memories, stories, and camaraderie are all elements of a successful bash. Note that those elements are all appropriate for creating an emotionally meaningful Ceremony.

Personal taste is exactly that—personal. A celebration of life should reflect the personality of the life that is gone. This means that a tone needs to be set for the Ceremony that reflects the individual and the personal taste of the surviving family members.

Religion

Religion is a touchy thing to talk about. I realize and support the notion that every religion has the right to determine its own rules and practices. Similarly, people have a right to determine their own beliefs and spiritual practices. None of my comments here are intended as criticism of any particular denomination. The remarks are presented only to help those who are "unchurched" to understand the wide range of practices they might confront.

The fact is that many families who are not currently affiliated with a church want to have some spiritual element as part of a Ceremony. That's okay; it's a very personal decision. The same decision is often made with regard to weddings. Somehow, in the course of celebrating these rites of passage, there is comfort in including an element of the familiar and inspirational. But families should only do what they are comfortable with. If you have religious beliefs (or needs), avoiding religion as a part of a Ceremony is just as wrong as being forced into a religious ritual if that is not wanted. Mortuaries should be able to help you have whatever elements of a Ceremony you feel are important.

If you and your family do not want organized religion to play a part, remember a mortuary should be able to help you develop the type of Ceremony you want. So don't settle for something that doesn't match your needs and beliefs. Note, however, that some mortuaries have strong affiliations to certain religious denominations. For example, Stewart Enterprises of New Orleans operates the mortuaries in the cemeteries owned by the Archdiocese of Los Angeles through a subsidiary named Catholic Mortuary Services.[1] Similarly, Sinai Temple owns Mount Sinai Memorial Park and Mortuary. It is reasonable to assume that mortuaries with strong religious affiliation exist for a specific purpose and may not be as flexible as those without such close ties to a specific denomination.

Clergy

Most active church members want their own pastors to conduct their Ceremonies. However, people with no church affiliation should not feel that asking a member of the clergy to conduct a Ceremony for them would seem hypocritical. Although I'm sure most members of the clergy would rather have you regularly attend their church services, many are willing to conduct Ceremonies when families are not members of a church. Most mortuaries keep a list of clergy in the area who are available to conduct Ceremonies for families without specific church affiliations.

Clergy are typically very busy, so it's a good idea to contact your priest, minister, rabbi, or other clergyperson before scheduling the day and time of the Ceremony. This is something that a mortuary will do for you as part of the process of arranging the Ceremony.

Clergy Honoraria

It's customary to give an honorarium to a clergyperson who offici- ates at a Ceremony. The honorarium recognizes the time spent with the family discussing and preparing for the Ceremony as well as the time spent in travel to meet with the family or to the Cer- emony. The amount of the honoraria is subjective. Your mortuary should be able to tell you what amount is typical in your area. If the clergyperson goes to extra efforts on your behalf, that effort also should be taken into consideration when determining the amount of the honoraria.

The family can give the honorarium directly to the clergyperson or ask the mortuary to take care of it as a "cash advance" item.

Music

It is said that music lifts the soul, so what could be more appropri- ate at a Ceremony than music? Music is such a large part of our lives that most families want it to be part of a Ceremony. Families need to decide how much music there should be, what music is wanted, and how it should be played.

When Ceremonies were primarily a rather inflexible reli- gious rite, music was generally somber hymns. A vocal soloist was sometimes used and an organ was the most common instrument.

However, times have changed. With the ready availability of very high quality music systems, it became common for music to be played from CDs. While live music is still popular and organs are still used often, organs are no longer the automatic choice. Bagpipers, guitars, harps, mariachi bands, pianos, string quartets, trumpets, violins, and a myriad of other instruments now make appearances at Ceremonies.

This is in line with the changes that have happened in music during many church services. Not only have the instruments changed, but so have the musical selections. Sure, hymns are still popular with many people, but quite often secular, inspirational music is used in conjunction with, or in place of, traditional hymns.

Not long ago, I attended the Ceremony for John. His family had decided to play Hawaiian music before the Ceremony because John loved Hawaii. Another man I knew chose the music he wanted played at his Ceremony. Leo chose a traditional religious piece, Mallot's "The Lord's Prayer," and "Walk On" from Rogers and Hammerstein's musical, *Carousel*.

Although some feel that times have changed, it must also be acknowledged that there are members of the clergy who believe that a Ceremony should only be a religious service dedicated to God. They hold that it's not about the deceased and that secular music is not appropriate. As one minister put it, people holding views that they should be able to have any music they want are reflecting "…humanistic, secular attitudes that are the true enemy of the Gospel."[2] If you have asked a mortuary to help you get a clergyperson, you should feel comfortable making sure that your needs are being met. If not, ask your funeral director to refer you to someone else.

Visitation

Sometimes called a "viewing," a visitation is an opportunity for people to pay their respects to the family of the deceased before the Ceremony. Most commonly, visitations are held in a mortuary with the deceased present. However, just having the deceased present doesn't mean that the casket has to be open (or closed, either). It's entirely up to personal preference.

Lying in state is a form of visitation. When John F. Kennedy was assassinated, thousands of people who had never met him filed past his closed casket, as he lay in state in the rotunda of the United States Capitol Building. These people were there because they felt some connection to him and his family. It was an expression of sorrow for many of them as well as an expression of support for the Kennedy family.

Some families want to be present during most of the scheduled visitation time to receive friends. Other families choose not to be present but take comfort in the notes and comments left by those who do attend. Many people find it especially important to attend a visitation when they will not be able to attend the Ceremony. Others who feel very close to the family or the deceased find the visitation an important part of the grieving process. Just as families often find the process of arranging a Ceremony to be a poignant moment of recognition that they have lost someone they have cared about, friends attending a visitation find that they, too, must begin to accept that they have lost someone.

When people have not seen the deceased for some time or the death is sudden or unexpected, going to a visitation can help bring reality to the loss and help them say goodbye.

Objects For Reflection

The goal in planning a Ceremony is to make it meaningful, to have it reflect the life and unique qualities of the deceased, and to say goodbye in a way that will ease the grieving process. There are as many ways to do this as you can conceive in your imagination. One of the ways of doing this is to use physical objects that are a reflection of the interests and personality of the deceased. They can be a powerful way of stimulating memories and helping those that attend understand and relate to the person who passed away. But, in the end, they are props used to stimulate memories and make the Ceremony more meaningful. They are a means to an end rather than an end unto themselves. With that said, here are some ideas about ways in which objects might be used to symbolize the various aspects of someone's life.

Memory Table

For the Ceremony, put together a collection of pictures, mementos, and other things that express the interests and personality of the deceased. Memory tables also can be used at a visitation.

If Aunt Jane was an ardent gardener, a memory table might have pictures of her favorite part of the garden and that funky old pair of rubber boots she wore when she was gardening. Or, it might include that fern plant she worked so hard to keep alive.

Perhaps Dad took up painting when he retired. How about bringing in some of his paintings, including that unfinished one he was working on? His painter's pallet and brushes also might be included.

Or maybe one of Granddad's proudest moments was when he won that football trophy in high school. Bring in the trophy and try to find some of the old press clippings.

Grandmother Julia was very proud of her grandchildren. Pictures of them—particularly ones with her—would tell or remind everyone attending the Ceremony something about her.

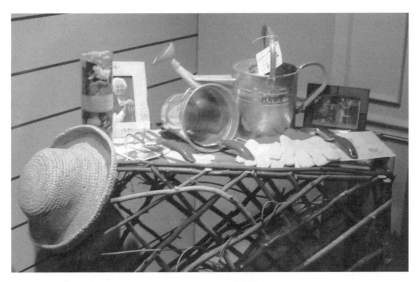

Figure 1. An example of a small memory table for a grandmother who loved to garden.

The idea is to think of things that represent what was important to the person and what they'd like to be remembered for. Photos, hobby items, awards, mementos, and souvenirs are only some of the things that could be used. The reflections and memories triggered by these things that are "just objects" are an effective way to bring friends and family together and to stimulate the sharing of their own memories and stories about the person they have loved.

Videos

A video has the potential for adding both impact and personalization to Ceremonies. More and more families have video cameras that they use to record significant family events. If you're happy with the quality of these, they can be a poignant part of a Ceremony. Still photos also can be combined into a sort of video slide show.

The caution is that we're all used to the very slick, fast paced, and heavily edited video of movies and TV. So make sure that the video you use is an appropriate length—short, probably not much more than five minutes—and is edited to keep it interesting to a diverse audience. This can be a lot of work but when done well, it is very memorable. There also are commercial services that will create a video montage from your still photos, adding appropriate background music for effect.

I recently attended a Ceremony that included a video montage done by one of the commercial services. The company that made the video put together a wonderful mixture from family still photos and added music that was appropriate for the family—Irish music in this case. Everyone at the service was moved by it. The video added an amazing personal touch to the Ceremony. If many of the firms that make these can regularly produce a result of this quality, I think videos will become much more common at Ceremonies.

Obituaries

An obituary is a notice or announcement that a death has taken place. Traditionally, these have been published in local newspapers and are distinguished from news stories about people who have passed away. Some papers publish short obituaries without charge while most charge for long, detailed notices. In urban areas, where there may be considerable overlap of local and regional newspapers, it's not always obvious where an obituary notice should be published. Although "home town" papers may publish obituary notices without charge, larger metropolitan newspapers tend to view an obituary notice as they do classified advertising and will charge by the line or by the word.

Most families assume that they will be able to contact those whom they feel would want to know about the death. To the extent that is true, an obituary notice may not be necessary. If they are unsure about their ability to contact people who are close to the family or to the deceased, then an obituary notice is a good way to let people know. Additionally, if there are many people to contact, the task may just be too overwhelming to do by phone. However, increased use of the Internet now makes it possible to "broadcast" a message to many people simultaneously.

The items that are most frequently included in an obituary notice are:

* The name of the deceased

* Date, time, and place of the visitation.

* Date, time, and place of the Ceremony.

A longer obituary notice will carry more biographical information about the deceased and may include:

* Names of spouse, children, and grandchildren.

* A short biographical statement that might include career highlights, organizations belonged to, honors, and so on.

The more that is included, the longer the obituary notice will be. And, thus, the higher the cost will be.

It's a good idea to have several people read the obituary

notice to determine what is missing. One family I know wrote a very long, personal obituary that they sent directly to the paper. Although they wanted a private Ceremony, they also wanted to have a visitation open to all their friends. Unfortunately, while they put in the time of the visitation, they forgot to put in the day or location! It was sad that almost no one came to the visitation. [suggest replacing "came to the visitation" with "attended." to reduce repetition]

Mini-Biographies

Just as some families like longer obituaries, some families now like to write mini-biographies to be included with the Ceremony program (sometimes called a memory folder). Families write these short biographies not only to tell the history of someone they loved, but also to tell something about who the person was. Many times pictures, poems, or other things are included that further personalize the mini-biographies. This personalization not only adds to the impact of the Ceremony, it also can be something to send friends and relatives who were not able to attend the service.

Casket at a Ceremony?

Although the question often posed is "Should the casket be present at a Ceremony?" the real question is whether the deceased should be present. There are several ways to look at this.

One way is from the point of view of religion. Some faiths believe that it's important (sometimes mandatory, with few exceptions) that the body of the deceased be present in the church for final rites. Other faiths are willing to have a Ceremony with or without the deceased being present.

If there aren't religious requirements, then the decision is more personal and philosophical. Having the deceased present is a tangible reminder that a death has occurred. This recognition is an important part of the grieving process. Some also would say that it may help focus the Ceremony on the deceased. On the other hand, there are those who feel that having the deceased present is "morbid." If cremation is chosen, an alternative to having the deceased present is to have the cremated remains present in an urn.

Whatever decision you or your family makes, if the deceased is not to be present, then I caution you to search your heart to make sure that the decision isn't motivated by attempting to avoid confrontation with the loss. Avoidance will not help you on your journey through the grieving process.

Open Or Closed Casket?

While most people believe it should be a family decision, there is some difference of opinion among clergy, psychologists, and sociologists about whether it's better for the casket to be open or closed at a Ceremony or visitation.

They almost all agree, however, that members of the immediate family should view the deceased at some time after death takes place. Doing so is considered a helpful and healing experience, and its value is widely documented in sociological and psychological studies on the subject. Some people find it difficult to accept the fact that death has occurred. Hearing about it from others is one thing, but seeing the direct evidence is quite another. Psychologists tell us that many family members find it hard to begin life again until they accept the fact that their loss is real and permanent, having seen so for themselves. Noted psychologist Dr. Theresa Rando said, "Viewing the body is often quite helpful, as it challenges your normal desire to deny the loss while promoting acceptance of the death."[3]

In addition, it can be beneficial to see the deceased in a casket, dressed in a favorite suit or gown, looking like he or she did before a final illness. This can help erase an unpleasant image and provide a more desirable "memory picture" of the deceased. Some people have a strong desire and need to see the person they have cared about—to spend a final moment with them. To them, bodies represent the physical part of life and death has separated them from that.

Some religious denominations require that the casket be closed at a Ceremony in the church but have no restrictions about an open casket in a mortuary visitation room.

Flowers Or Contributions To Charity?

Families sometimes ask that contributions be made to charitable organizations in lieu of sending flowers. Although many charities promote this, it is yet another decision that should be based on the family's wishes.

Why send flowers? The atmosphere of a Ceremony with flowers as symbols of life and beauty is far different from a stark, plain Ceremony. Flowers are a way for friends and family to show they care. In a time when friends are often spread out over large distances, sending flowers is an expression of caring that does make an impact, particularly when they can't be there themselves. Many people seem to be reluctant or ashamed to send contributions as small as the cost of flowers. Others just never get around to it. One of my friends was rather cynical about the impact of flowers, until his father passed away. The Ceremony was held on the East Coast, so his West Coast friends did not attend. However, he told me after he returned home that the flowers received from friends who could not physically be there had a tremendous impact on him. He felt a closeness to them and that they were reaching out to him.

Sending flowers to Ceremonies meets some very special needs. Friends find it to be a convenient and appropriate way to express their sympathy. At a time when some feel words to be inadequate, flowers are a gift that is symbolic of caring.

On the other hand, flowers are perishable. They are seen at the visitation, Ceremony, and at the burial site. The family may take a few plants or arrangements with them. With the short time flowers may last, people sometimes wonder if it wouldn't be better to contribute to a particular charity in the name of the deceased—a donation that would benefit humanity and, consequently, have a most lasting effect.

There is some merit to both views. Personally, I favor having flowers because I think it's more personal. When my mother passed away, I received a card from a charity on the other side of the country telling me that a business colleague had made a contribution in her name. The organization would have been meaningless to my mother (and our family), and we didn't have any association with the town where the charity was located. Perhaps I am cynical, but I was left with the impression that the donation was done for that colleague's benefit—to gain stature with the charity rather than any real thought of it being meaningful or supportive to our grieving family.

What Happens to the Flowers After the Ceremony?

Occasionally, people wonder what happens to the flowers that are sent to a Ceremony. Generally, the flowers go to the place of burial, but sometimes the family will choose a few arrangements or plants and take them home.

Periodically, mortuaries are asked to donate flowers that were used in Ceremonies to churches or for decorations of various sorts. Forest Lawn's response has always been, "We can't do that. They don't belong to us." Friends and family send flowers to the Ceremony and I do not believe a mortuary or cemetery has a right to give them away. Any family that wants to do something with the flowers is free to do so, but it's not right for someone else to make that decision for them.

Some mortuaries take the position that the flowers are a gift to the deceased, and as a result, no one should be able to take them away. To me, that seems like hard stance to take, but it happens. 🍁

6. Cremation

Practiced in Asia for thousands of years, cremation was seldom used in the United States until the twentieth century. Its popularity, however, has grown in recent years, particularly on the West Coast. Although the popular media often makes it seem as though there has been a rapid shift to cremation, in reality in most areas it has been only a slow but steady change in acceptance. Today, cremation is an option available through nearly every mortuary.

Often when people talk about "cremation," they are using the word as shorthand for practical, no-frills, no-service disposition. In coastal areas, including Southern California, "cremation" is often understood to mean cremation with disposal at sea. Although cremation can be followed by a low cost, "practical" disposition, there is no requirement that this be the case. Indeed, some families who choose cremation spend more than they might on a traditional Ceremony and burial. Families choose cremation for many reasons, and many choose it specifically because they feel cremation gives them more options and more control.

Families who decide to cremate often hold a Ceremony and have a family memorial in a cemetery. Cremated remains may be memorialized in many ways—ground burial (either in a full-sized space or a smaller cremation space), indoor or outdoor columbarium, mausoleum crypts, or other private memorials. Some families take home the urn containing the cremated remains, while other families choose to have the cremated remains scattered. Scattering should be considered carefully, because it's a once-and-for-all, cannot-be-undone decision. Once cremated remains are scattered, their retrieval is impossible.

Cremation can take place before or after a Ceremony. When the cremation follows the Ceremony, the deceased is often present at the Ceremony and a casket is used. When cremation precedes the Ceremony and the family wants to have the cremated remains present, an urn containing the remains is at the Ceremony. In many cases, those who choose to memorialize their loved one at a service may require a casket in addition to the urn. While the actual cremation itself is an added expense, the total cost may be somewhat less because the price of the smaller cemetery space or niche may be less than that of a burial space or mausoleum crypt that is large enough for a full-sized casket.

A 1995 study by The Wirthlin Group—and a 1999 update of that study—showed that Americans were increasingly likely to choose cremation.[1] The interesting thing was that people were more likely to accept cremation for themselves than for someone they love. Often what they said in effect was, "It doesn't matter what happens to me; I'll be dead." However, they did not have such a cavalier attitude about someone they love.

A Process, Not An End

Many people say "I want cremation" thinking that is the only decision they will have to make. That isn't so. Cremation is only a process. The process of cremation, described later, changes a full sized body into a smaller quantity of cremated remains. Although the body is in a different form, you must still make a decision about what to do with the cremated remains—scatter them somewhere, bury them in a cemetery, or take them home.

Some people think of cremation as a practical or pragmatic disposition—no fuss, no muss, no hassles, and no decisions; just get it over with. In reality, this isn't quite true. Actually, people choosing cremation have even more options than are available to people who choose traditional Ceremonies and burial. Deciding upon cremation doesn't decrease the number of decisions that must be made; having a cremation may actually increase the number of decisions to be made.

Cremation With A Ceremony

Choosing cremation doesn't mean that there will not be a Ceremony. With cremation, there can be a traditional Ceremony with the deceased present, a Ceremony with an urn containing the cremated remains present, or a memorial service. Cremation does not take away the opportunity for a meaningful Ceremony that helps family and friends share the experience of loss and celebrate the life of someone they knew and loved.

The 1999 update of the Wirthlin study found that better than 80 percent of people who said they would choose cremation also wanted some form of Ceremony.[2] All of the reasons for having some sort of Ceremony are just as valid with a cremation as when there is not a cremation. A Ceremony that allows you to say goodbye your way is entirely possible and appropriate with a cremation.

More Options

As mentioned earlier, families choosing cremation actually have more options than families choosing traditional burial. Cremated remains can be buried, placed in an above ground crypt or columbarium niche, scattered, or taken home. A variety of containers can hold cremated remains—from simple sheet metal or plastic boxes to urns made of bronze, marble, or other materials.

Figure 2. Urns for cremated remains are available in a wide range of prices, styles, and materials. *Photo from Forest Lawn Mortuary*

Some manufacturers now offer pieces of sculpture that are also urns.

Here are a few options available to those choosing cremation that are not available otherwise:

* Take the cremated remains home in a suitable urn.

* Split or divide the cremated remains into multiple urns or "keepsakes," so all members of the family can feel close to the deceased

* Scattering (even in more than one place)

* Shoot a portion of the remains into space

* Make a portion of the cremated remains into jewelry

Urns And Keepsakes

A wide variety of materials are used to make urns. Many think of urns as being vase-like containers of bronze. However, now there are many more choices of styles and materials. Some urns are sculptures that have a space in the base for cremated remains, others are hand crafted wood boxes, and still others are made of fine ceramics.

In addition to the wide variety of urns, keepsakes of various sorts are widely available. Keepsakes can be pieces of jewelry or small statues that have space for a small portion of the cremated remains. Sometimes family members do not all share the same opinion about whether or not it's "proper" to split or divide the cremated remains of someone they love. I personally am not comfortable with splitting cremated remains—it may be irrational, but I'd like all of my parts (other than organ donations) to end up together. Nevertheless, I respect the right of any family to make a choice, provided all of the proper family members authorize splitting the cremated remains.

Scattering

Scattering needs to be considered carefully for several reasons. The concerns expressed here are not meant to discourage scattering, but to put it into some perspective.

First, scattering is irreversible. This is true wherever the cremated remains are scattered. If it's in the ocean or another body of water, it's obvious why the deed can't be undone. That doesn't make it a bad or wrong decision, just one that shouldn't be taken lightly. If in doubt, wait—it can be done later. At the time you've lost someone you love, you shouldn't be making hasty decisions about anything, scattering included.

Second, be careful where it's done. There are laws that differ from state to state about where it's legal to scatter. Generally, it's not legal to scatter cremated remains on private property without the owner's permission. This is true whether it's a cemetery or a residential backyard. Laws vary about permissibility of scattering on public property. For anyone wanting to do scattering at sea, the requirement is to go three miles offshore and within thirty days of scattering file a report with the U.S. Environmental Protection Agency.[3] If you are doing this yourself, check with local authorities to find out if your state or local government has additional requirements for permits or filings. Mortuaries, and individuals that scatter cremated remains at sea on their behalf, are required by many states to have government issued licenses and must comply with all government requirements. If you scatter without obtaining appropriate permits and making required filings, you could be charged with violations of the law.

Third, and perhaps most importantly, try to project how you will feel in the future about the irreversible scattering. Many grief counselors have worked with people who scattered their loved ones cremated remains and later came to have a sense of unease and regret about their decision. This regret isn't universal, but there is enough anecdotal evidence to underscore the irreversible nature of scattering and to encourage soul searching to avoid potential regret later.

I recently ran into Mary, a widow who had lost her husband last year. Paul was an avid golfer and had expressed a desire to be cremated and have his cremated remains scattered at six different golf courses. Mary told me she wanted to come to Forest Lawn to make arrangements for herself and to get "some sort of plaque" to remember Paul. Today, many families that choose scattering also choose to have a permanent memorial at a cemetery. Sometimes this decision is made at the time of the cremation, but it also can be made at a later date. A plaque or memorial to remember someone who isn't buried at that place is called a cenotaph.

So, do some soul searching before scattering. Not scattering doesn't mean that you have to buy cemetery property immediately. You can take the cremated remains home and give the decision some time. If, after a while, you are still comfortable with scattering, then go ahead. The important thing is to be cautious about actions that are irreversible, because you could change your mind. A previous section stressed the importance of talking about death and funeral arrangements. Well, that same concept applies here. Talk to family members about this. Ask them if they feel they need a place to visit that represents the person they have loved. Examine your feelings before you proceed.

Description Of Cremation Process

Although the following disclosure may, at first reading, seem insensitive or even unpleasant, it is factual. The romantic notion of cremation resulting in fluffy ashes that can be lifted to the sky by a gust of wind is entirely wrong. Cremated remains are not ashes, and they are not fluffy. To correct the popular misconception and avoid misunderstanding by consumers, California now requires the following statement on all cremation authorizations and includes the description in its "Consumer Guide to Funeral and Cemetery Purchases" which mortuaries and cemeteries are required to give all consumers. Not all states require statements similar to this one.

The human body burns with the casket, container or other material in the cremation chamber. During the cremation, the contents of the chamber may be moved to facilitate incineration. The chamber is composed of ceramic or other material which disintegrates slightly during each cremation and the product of that disintegration is commingled with the cremated remains. Nearly all of the contents of the cremation chamber, consisting of the cremated remains, disintegrated chamber material, and small amounts of residue from previous cremations, are removed together and crushed, pulverized, or ground to facilitate inurnment or scattering. Some residue remains in the cracks and uneven places in the chamber. Periodically, the accumulation of this residue is removed and interred in a dedicated cemetery property, or scattered at sea.[4]

Crematories also require removal of pacemakers before a cremation takes place because the devices often explode with the intense heat in a crematory retort.

The Right Cremated Remains?

Because of the nature of the process, you really are relying on the integrity of the crematory you are dealing with as far as making sure the cremated remains returned to you are those of the person you loved. If you have any doubt, ask the crematory if they will let you witness placement of the casket or container in the cremation chamber. If not, ask "Why?" For safety reasons—noise, hot equipment, and so on—few crematories will let you witness the entire process. But that shouldn't stop you from asking a crematory what their procedures are for ensuring the integrity of the cremation process and that each family receives the correct cremated remains.

As an example of procedures that can help maintain the integrity of identification, let me summarize some of what Forest Lawn does. As each deceased is brought to one of our mortuaries, he or she is assigned a unique identification number. This unique number is stamped on a thick steel disk that stays with the deceased at all times—regardless of what options are chosen: burial, cremation, or shipping to another cemetery. The material the disk is made from was chosen because even after going through the cremation process the unique identification number will remain legible. After cremation and processing of the cremated remains, the disk is placed in the urn with the cremated remains. We also have various logs and other documentation to ensure the integrity of the process. However, this is certainly not the only way to ensure correct identification of cremated remains. Some crematories will have similar procedures, while others will have developed different methods that they believe are appropriate.

Facilities that have well thought out plans and procedures will be more than willing to tell you about their operations and what safeguards they have in place. If they've put a lot of effort into establishing reliable means of handling cremations, they will want you to know how seriously they view their responsibility.

Crematories

Over the years, there has been a lot of publicity about cremation scandals. While it's true that some terrible things have occurred, the majority of crematories are sound, ethical operators. Nonetheless, cremation buyers should know how to choose a crematory that they can rely on.

Many of the problems we've heard about have involved third party crematories—crematories that perform cremations for a number of independent mortuaries. Because cremation facilities are expensive, some mortuaries cannot justify the investment in a cremation facility of their own. So they will subcontract the actual cremations to another company. Ask the mortuary if the cremations it sells are performed by the mortuary's own employees in facilities it owns.

If the mortuary does use a third party crematory, ask for more information about the it. How long have has it been in business? Where is the crematory located? Has the management of the mortuary visited the facility? When was the last visit or inspection made? What is the crematory like? Is the mortuary aware of any problems with it? Once you know the name of the facility, you also can contact your state's crematory regulatory agency to find out if the crematory has a history of consumer complaints, has a valid license, or has been cited for violations of the law.

Regardless of ownership, not all crematories operate under the same philosophy. Broadly speaking, there are two extremes.

At one end of the spectrum are the crematories that are primarily concerned with providing low cost, practical disposition. Their facilities will tend to be Spartan and often are located in industrial or other low cost areas.

At the other end are crematories that are most concerned with dignified, respectful handling of the deceased. They even may have facilities designed to allow families to witness the beginning of the cremation process. Of course, providing the respectful, reverent and careful handling of each deceased coupled with a crematory facility that is more upscale does cost more to operate, so their prices often may not be the lowest.

Neither of these operating philosophies is good or bad. The important point here is that there are different approaches to operating a crematory. Many years ago, Forest Lawn decided that it would not try to compete for cremations on price. It's important to us to treat each deceased with the respect and reverence that each cremation deserves. Our culture is to remember that each deceased was a father, mother, child, or sibling who was loved and important to someone else. We're fanatical about performing each cremation with care and providing respectful care for each deceased.

Shipping Cremated Remains

Although cremated remains are not hazardous, not all common carriers are willing to transport them. This is primarily due to a fear of litigation if they should happen to misplace or damage them rather than from sensibility about handling a box with cremated remains in it. At the time this was written, the most common means of shipping cremated remains within the United

States was as certified mail through the United States Postal Service. United Parcel Service[5] and FedEx[6] would not allow sending cremated remains using their services.

The reason for using some form of certified mail or express mail by the Post Office is that letters and packages sent that way receive individualized tracking while regular parcel post does not. The assumption is that this special handling will result in fewer mistakes. When mistakes do occur, the package can be located and the mistake corrected.

You also may carry cremated remains with you on a common carrier—bus, plane, or train. However, you may need to have a permit for disposition or similarly titled document accompanying the cremated remains. 🍁

Planning for Goodbye

A Scot's Farewell

When I come to the end of the road,
And the sun has set for me,
I want no tears in a gloom-filled room,
Why cry for a soul set free?
Miss me a little but not for long,
And not with your head bowed low.
Remember the love that we once shared
Miss me...but let me go....
When you are lonely and sick of heart,
Go the friend we know,
And bury your sorrows in doing good
    deeds,
Miss me...but let me go.

Source unknown

7. Why Prearrange?

Most of us are very aware of the need to plan for major events in life. We see a lot of advertising that focuses on financial planning—buying a car or house, putting the kids through college, and saving for retirement. The common message with each of these is that if we plan well we can accomplish our goals and get to enjoy our success. If the plans don't work out quite right, we bear the responsibility for that and the burden for correcting the situation. Unfortunately, when it comes to the end of our lives, we don't have a chance to "make it right" if we don't plan. The government has decided how our estates will be divided if we don't have a will. It also has decided who gets to determine what our Ceremonies will be like and where we will be buried if we don't do something ahead of time.

Prearrangement is the way many people plan for the Ceremonies that will mark the end of their lives. Prearrangement, as discussed in more detail in the next chapter, is a combination of writing down your wishes for your Ceremony and providing some means for paying for it.

There are many reasons people prearrange. The reasons

run from very rational thoughts to those that are more emotion-based. Some people want to control what their Ceremony will be like. They might not want the family to spend more than a certain amount or might not want their heirs to cut back on the Ceremony to get the money for themselves. Although the latter may seem odd to most of us, greed does come out at odd times. In some states, if you prearrange your Ceremony, the prearrangements can be locked in—no one can change them.[1] If you want to create prearrangements that cannot be altered, talk to your local mortuary and ask them what can be done in your state to accomplish this objective.

Common Reasons

Here are some common reasons people mention when asked why they want to prearrange:

* To have the peace of mind that comes from selecting the type of Ceremony they want ahead of their death and making the decisions together with their spouse or significant other.

* To ease the emotional burden on their family at the time of their death by having decisions made ahead of time.

* To avoid questions about what they "would have wanted."

* To avoid financial burdens on their family.

* To "lock-in" today's prices by buying guaranteed delivery of specified goods and services for a Ceremony.

* To make sure the Ceremony is just as simple or elaborate as they want it to be—to make sure no one can change the Ceremony they specify.

* To set aside money for final expenses that does not count against them in qualifying for some kinds of government benefits.

Change When Decisions Are Made

When faced with the loss of someone they love, many people do not know what to do, as they are dealing with grief and other emotions that make it difficult to make decisions. Nevertheless, decisions must be made. Widows talk of not knowing what their husbands would have wanted. Widowers wonder what is right. Children wish Mom or Dad had told them what they wanted. Prearrangement is the way to dramatically reduce the number of decisions that must be made when a death occurs. It helps people avoid having to make many choices while under stress and coping with the loss of someone close.

Talk About This, Too

I believe there is great value in the peace of mind that can come from making prearrangements. However, ask yourself whose peace of mind you are concerned with—besides your own, of course.

A lady recently told me about her 85-year-old uncle expressing a desire to be cremated, to have no Ceremony of any type, and to have the cremated remains scattered someplace. As she discussed this with him, she told him that the family might want to have a Ceremony because it was important to them as survivors. He was somewhat taken aback by this, as he hadn't considered things from the family's point of view. They ended up agreeing on what kind of Ceremony would meet everyone's wishes. But if they hadn't talked about it, there would have just been a cremation with no Ceremony because he had already signed up with a no-frills, no-service cremation society.

Prearrangements need to be talked about. Sure, give precedence to your wishes for yourself, but also consider of the needs of your family and friends as well. ✱

8. How To Prearrange

The best alternative to making decisions at the time of death is to make them ahead of time. Making decisions in advance provides a level of comfort in knowing that the decisions were ones reached together, without the stress of coping with the emotional turmoil that comes with the death of someone you have loved. Although this may be an oversimplification, you have three choices:

* Do nothing.

* Write down your wishes for your Ceremony.

* Prearrange your ceremony.

It's clear what the "do nothing" option means. You leave the decisions about your burial, Ceremony, or cremation to your survivors. Having no direction from you, they won't know what you might have wanted. They may overspend, or they may take the lowest price they can find.

Just writing down your wishes is a big help to your family and survivors. For some, that is enough. Others want to do everything possible and do not feel they've taken care of everything until they have completed a prearrangement.

Once you've decided that you'd like to prearrange, you then need to decide how you want to do it. You can best make that decision by understanding the options available to you. Putting money aside for a Ceremony as part of a prearrangement is not like putting money in a savings account, so it's important to understand what you are trying to accomplish before making a decision.

The terminology related to prearrangement isn't consistent. Not only are there many terms that can be used, different people use the same term to mean different things. You may hear terms like prearrange, prefinance, preneed purchase, prepaid funeral, preplan, and so on. To try to keep this simple, I'm only going to use two terms:

Writing down your wishes. This is making a decision about what you want your Ceremony to be like and recording those wishes in writing.

Prearrangement. This includes writing down your wishes as well as having some form of financing in place to carry out those wishes.

Writing down your wishes is something that many couples do together. Often getting or updating a will triggers doing this. The most important aspect of the process is the discussion that goes with it. The conversation can bring people closer together whether they are children, parents, siblings, spouses, or other partners. Documenting your wishes in writing can even help avoid disputes when death occurs.

After putting your wishes in writing, the next step is to decide if you should prearrange by setting funds aside for final expenses. Some like to go through the process of writing down their wishes before making the decision to prearrange. Others are more comfortable just jumping into the financial side of things. Before getting into a discussion about prearrangement and various ways to prearrange, I want to define three more terms to make the discussion more manageable:

Seller. For purposes of the prearrangement discussion, a "Seller" is the person who sells the prearrangement. As described later, a prearrangement is generally a Financial Tool combined with your wishes being written down. A variety of organizations can do this—mortuaries, cemeteries, crematories, retail casket stores, and insurance agents—subject to what state laws allow. Rather than keep reciting this long list, the term "Seller" will refer to all of them.

Provider. A "Provider" is an organization that actually delivers the goods and merchandise that are part of the prearrangement. Possible providers include mortuaries, cemeteries, crematories, retail casket stores, and monument dealers. Not all of these can provide everything, so the term as used here means a company or organization that legally can provide the goods and services. Just as with the term Seller, the term "Provider" will be used for all rather than trying to use the long list or qualify which organizations can provide what. In other parts of the book, there are descriptions of what the various Providers can provide.

Financial Tool. The financial aspect of most prearrangement involves putting money aside for final expenses. This can be done in several ways including insurance, trusts, and bank savings accounts. Each of these possible methods is discussed later, but to discuss the broad topic of prearrangement, these are all lumped together as "Financial Tools."

Prearranging

It is necessary to start with some explanation of the items that might be included in prearrangement. Many Providers sell both goods and services. However, there is some overlap in what goods and services the various Providers might sell that is determined by state restrictions and local customs.

The term "goods and services" includes all items that might be part of a ceremony. The "goods" portion includes things like caskets, flowers, urns, memorials, outer burial containers, programs, and visitation books. "Services" include the basic service fee of the mortuary, embalming or refrigeration, mortuary professional care, and cemetery burial charges. A more comprehensive listing of goods and services can be found in Appendix B. Most of the goods and services cannot be delivered until death occurs, and are the items that generally are purchased or provided for in a prearrangement. There are a few things, though, like cemetery burial rights, that can be conveyed ahead of time by a deed or certificate of burial right. Accordingly, the discussion in this section is primarily about the goods and services that may be part of a Ceremony.

The decision to purchase goods or services before time of death involves financial as well as subjective factors. The first thing to understand is that there are many ways of setting aside funds for a funeral, burial, or cremation. Although many think they are buying a Ceremony ahead of time that often is not the case. What people usually do is buy some sort of Financial Tool to put money aside. When death occurs, the Financial Tool is redeemed to provide funds for the purchase of goods and services.

Each of the methods of putting funds aside has its strengths

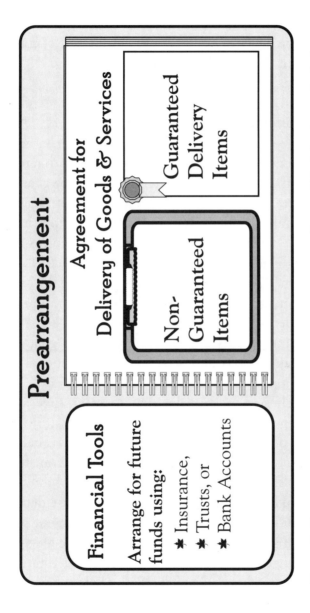

Figure 3. There are two major components to prearrangement: a Financial Tool that is a method of providing funds, and Writing Down Your Wishes that is a list of what you want for your Ceremony. There will be a "statement of goods and services" that indicates which items have guaranteed delivery and which items will only receive an allocation of available funds from the Financial Tool.

and weaknesses, sometimes more of one than the other. When setting funds aside, you need to understand what you your commitment is to the Seller as well as knowing what sort of contractual commitment the Seller has to you.

Price Or Delivery Guarantee

Often there is loose talk of "price guarantees" in relation to pre-arrangements. However, it is unusual for a true price guarantee to be part of the Financial Tool. Generally, a prearrangement includes a second agreement that is a commitment on the part of a Provider to deliver the specified goods and services in exchange for the value of the Financial Tool at the time of death. Although this may seem like a technicality, it is significant because the delivery guarantee usually is only valid if you use the specified Provider.

Most prearrangements should be thought of as "guaranteed delivery of specific goods and services at no additional cost" rather than calling them price guarantees.

Many purchasers make a decision to prearrange a Ceremony based upon a desire to lock-in the cost. They want to transfer all risk of price increases to another party—usually the Provider of the goods and services. In addition to transferring that risk to the Provider, they also get the peace of mind that comes from making the decisions and putting those decisions in writing. Although the result of the prearrangement mostly accomplishes this, it is important to understand the mechanics of your prearrangement—how it really works and what really happens. What does happen is that a Seller helps you set aside funds using a Financial Tool, and, in a separate agreement, a

Provider agrees to deliver certain things in exchange for the future value of that Financial Tool.

By now, you probably see some of the important distinctions between Sellers and Providers. The Seller's function is performed when the prearrangement is made. They set up the Financial Tool and help you write down your wishes. In most states, they turn over the money they receive to an insurance company, bank, or trust[,] less amounts that state regulations may allow them to keep to cover expenses. At the time of death, the funds in the Financial Tool then are turned over to the Provider. In cases where the Seller and Provider are the same, the distinction between the two is unimportant. However, if they are not the same, as a consumer you should understand that and ask questions about each.

Things To Think About

Here are some things to consider when deciding if prearrangement is right for you.

Is there a guaranteed delivery of everything covered by the contract? Usually the answer to this is "no," as some of the items cannot be determined easily ahead of time. The items that are not included in delivery guarantees are often cash advance items like clergy honoraria, obituaries, soloists, and services provided by third parties (someone other than the Provider). Additionally, some amounts will be allowances, as for flowers, where there are seasonal price fluctuations that make it difficult to reasonably specify what will be delivered in the future. Do not assume that all items have delivery guarantees. Some Providers will guarantee only the delivery of the casket but not the services. Other Providers will do the reverse. Still others will guarantee delivery of almost everything. If you're going to prearrange, make sure not only that you understand what the delivery guarantee applies to, but that your written agreement covers your understanding of what you will get.

What happens if the proceeds from the Financial Tool are more than the price of the goods and services at the time of death? Some Providers take the not unreasonable position that if they take the risk of costs rising faster than prices that they should get all the funds, even if the Financial Tool proceeds are greater than the list prices in place when the services are delivered. Others, either because they think it's right or because of statutory requirements, only take the lesser of the charges at list prices when the services are delivered or the amount of the Financial Tool. In this latter case, the consumer doesn't have to put up any more for the guaranteed items and may get money back.

Is the Seller also the Provider—does the Seller have the ability to deliver? Some Sellers of prearrangements rely on other Providers to deliver the Ceremonies. For example, a general insurance agency can sell an insurance policy for final expenses. But it's not really a prearrangement unless there also is an agreement with a Provider to deliver specified goods and services in the future. If the insurance agency is not also a licensed mortuary, owner of a mortuary, or other state-licensed Provider, the agency, as Seller, could not actually deliver the Ceremony. It would have to rely on a third party to be the Provider. Another example would be cremation. In California, only a firm with a crematory license can perform a cremation. As few mortuaries also have a crematory license, many mortuaries rely on other companies to perform cremations. An informed consumer should understand what goods and services are going to be delivered by the specified Provider and what goods and services will be delivered by third parties. Later sections discuss what may happen if you move or want to cancel.

How secure are the funds? The level and method of providing protection for the funds varies by type of Financial Tool.

As consumer groups have pointed out, prearrangement isn't an investment; it is a purchase. So you must realize that canceling a prearrangement may involve some sort of penalty. The penalty may be an actual loss of money in the form of a cancellation fee or it may be a penalty in the form of having the funds tied up until you die. These drawbacks are discussed under each of the prearrangement Financial Tools. The following information is presented to facilitate making decisions because informed consumers can make the best decisions about what is right for them. However, the specifics offered by any Seller or the requirements of your state laws may have an impact on your purchase. Ask plenty of questions!

AARP (formerly known as American Association of Retired People) encourages people to document their wishes but not to prearrange. They seem to focus on providing financing for final arrangements as a financial transaction and ignore the reality that most people prearrange Ceremonies ahead of time for peace of mind rather than financial reasons. To many, the financial advantages are just an additional benefit.

One aspect of AARP's concern that makes sense, though, is their interest in whether or not consumers get what they pay for. This is the same caveat that applies to many consumer transactions. Know whom you are dealing with. Since most hope they won't be using their prearrangement for some time, the history and stability of the Provider is quite important. Ask the Seller how long the Provider has been in business and if it is also the Provider or if it must rely on some third party. If the Seller must rely on an unrelated Provider, will the Seller step in and protect you, the buyer, if the Provider is unable to deliver as promised?

Financial Tools

Once you decide to put money away for a Ceremony, you must decide which is the best way for you. In simple terms, there are two conceptual methods of setting aside funds as part of a prearrangement—trusts and insurance. The details of how each of these works varies from state to state and not all states allow both methods for prearranging. Some states allow escrow accounts, either in addition to trusts or instead of trusts. Although there may be some legal differences between fund escrows and trusts, conceptually the two are similar. Therefore, only trusts will be covered here.

Start with answering a basic question: Does it make sense to you to put money aside for a Ceremony? Next, do you have the funds to do so in a lump sum or would it be better for you to finance the prearrangement with monthly payments? Hopefully, the following discussion will help you sort through the benefits and drawbacks of each of the options available to you. There are risks, of course, in just about every type of financial transaction. So you should make your own evaluation of the financial risk for any pre-arrangement method you are considering.

In addition to deciding what method of prearrangement financing to use, if you have a choice, you also should understand what other consumer protections may be in place in your state. The most common consumer issues relate to cancellation of prearrangements.[1] So you should know what the consequences would be if you decide to back out of a prearrangement. Knowing how the Seller's guarantee works is also important to understanding the ramifications of a cancellation.

Insurance

Insurance companies are regulated at the state level. Generally, each state has some authority over all sellers of insurance in their state, even when the insurance company is located in another state. Additionally, most states require insurance agents to take examinations to qualify for licensing before they can make sales. Agents also must work for a general agent or broker who has responsibility for an agent's actions.

Insurance products themselves are quite portable. If you own the policy, you control the proceeds and can determine how they are used. If you decide you don't want to use the original specified Provider, you probably will have to forgo the delivery guarantee, but you can go to another Provider and determine what you can purchase for the policy proceeds. Most of the insurance products used for prearranging today usually have some sort of clause that provides for the amount of the policy or death benefit to increase from year to year.

As far as cancellation goes, don't expect to get all your money back if you cancel. The insurance company sets its prices based upon the expectation that it will earn an investment return for a certain period of time. That investment return allows it to cover its costs of selling, administration, and profit in addition to paying the death benefit. If that period is cut short by your decision to cancel, the policy's provisions usually will provide for some penalty.

Insurance can seem quite complicated, so you shouldn't hesitate to ask questions of your insurance agent regarding how the policy works. Ask what happens if there is a death before all the premiums are paid, what happens if you move, what happens if you live to be 100, how do you know the insurance company is sound, how long have they been in business, and so on. Give it a little thought and you'll come up with the questions that are important to you.

How Insurance Works

When an insurance policy is the method for financing a prearrangement, it's helpful to understand the principles of how insurance operates, so you can better understand the benefits and restrictions of using insurance for prearrangement funding.

Life insurance is unlike auto insurance in that everyone will die. This is in contrast to an auto policy where it's assumed that only a small percentage of policyholders will have accidents or have their cars stolen.

In the case of life insurance, the insurance company's actuaries determine the average life expectancy of people. The company also estimates what it can earn from investing premium dollars between the time they are received and when death will occur. These investments are regulated by law. From these two variables, an insurance company determines what its premiums will be. All this assumes that the number of people insured will be quite large, so the estimates of average age at death will be accurate.

When people who have life insurance don't live as long as the actuaries expect, the life insurance company may fall short in the amount it has earned on the premiums paid. On the other hand, when people live longer than the expected average age, the company should have earned more on the money as premiums than it projected. The insurance company takes the risk of a death occurring before expected. It takes a great many policies for this to work out for the insurance company, for some people live shorter than expected and others live longer. The life insurance company makes its profit from earnings on investments and making accurate estimates of how long people will live. Actually, it's a lot more complicated than this because there are other provisions in the policies that affect pricing—cash surrender amounts, lump sum premium versus payments made over a period of time, and so on.

Some consumers ask why they can't get back all the money they've paid in premiums. Well, during the early years of the policy, the company doesn't have it. In the case of an insurance policy where the premiums are paid over a number of years, the company has probably paid out more money the first year than it has received in premiums. The money has gone to pay commissions and the cost of setting up the policy, so the insurance company would lose money by refunding everything. If they did that very often, they'd soon run out of money and undermine the security of the money of those who didn't try to get refunds.

Some insurance policies have a "cash surrender" value, meaning the policy can be turned in for a specified amount of money. It allows the company to make what it determines is a fair return on the effort it has engaged in, but is less than the insurance company has earned on the premium dollars. For example, some years ago, I took out a $10,000 whole life insurance policy. The annual premium was $170. After 20 years—and $3,400 in premium payments—the policy had a cash value of $3,220.

There also is a "paid-up" amount on some policies, where premiums are scheduled to be paid over time. This comes into play when a consumer stops making premium payments. This paid-up amount is the amount of life insurance the policy can be converted to if premium payments stop and is less than the policy's original face amount. When this is available, it usually is shown on a schedule in the policy[,] as are cash surrender values.

Trusts

One common method of financing prearrangements is to put money in trust. As individual states have different requirements, it is only possible to cover the principles of how these trusts operate. If you are considering a trust, you will want to ask questions about how the trust works in your state.

Figure 4. A typical relationship between premiums paid and insurance value for a whole life policy used for prearrangement. Note: This is only an example; actual results will vary by insurance issuer, law, and regulations as well as the age and health of the insured.

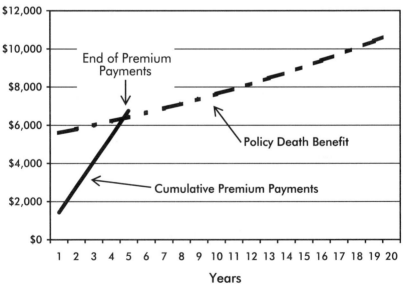

The general concept is easy: a consumer selects goods and services to be included in a prearrangement. Depending upon the relationship between the Seller and Provider, as well as state law, the prearrangement/trust agreement will cover how the trust operates and what will happen at time of death.

The Seller usually is required by state law to put some or all of the proceeds into a trust to ensure that funds will be available to purchase those goods and services from a Provider when death occurs. As with insurance, trust prearrangements are usually a Financial Tool combined with a guaranteed delivery of selected goods and services.

From the consumer's perspective, the establishment of the trust account provides some protection—unless the consumer changes his or her mind. Some trusts cannot be cancelled at all (they are irrevocable). Other trusts may have financial penalties for withdrawing funds for any purpose other than the purchase of goods and services. A few consumer groups have been quite critical of the cancellation fees, but I think that is probably not fair. The Seller of the prearrangement incurred costs related to that sale. In most cases, it took the financial risk of its costs rising faster than the amount invested in the trust. So the issue should probably be "What is a fair cancellation or withdrawal fee?" rather than the issue of whether or not there should be a fee.

Some states, like California, require 100 percent of the amount of the sale to be put in trust. Sellers can recoup some of their selling and administrative costs from earnings of the trust. Other states allow Sellers to keep a portion of the amount paid in by purchasers and only trust a portion of the amount of the sale. One method of doing this, as used in New Jersey, is to require that 60 percent of the retail price of the goods and services be put in trust. Another method, used in Michigan, is to require 130 percent of the cost of the cemetery merchandise (vaults and memorials) be put in trust. Each state has different trusting requirements.

If less money is put in the trust, then there is less protection for the consumer. If the business should fail, it might be hard to find another mortuary willing to deliver the goods and services for the amount in the trust. To the extent that the Seller can re-coup selling expenses from the trust or charge a revocation fee, a smaller amount may be available if the original Seller isn't the one to deliver the services. In short, the trust may not be as portable as an insurance policy.

Although there may be cancellation fees or administrative expenses, most trusts do have provisions for cancellation. That means that a consumer can change his or her mind in the future and at least get some of the money back.

Another issue relative to funeral goods and service trusts is: Who pays the taxes on the earnings of the trust? At one time, it was common for purchasers to receive IRS form 1099s each year and to have to declare the earnings of the trust as income. In some cases, this is no longer an issue as the taxes on the earnings are either paid by the trust or by the Seller to avoid irritating customers.

Before agreeing to use a trust for prearrangement financing, make sure you understand how it will work. Note that as most states have different licensing laws for cemeteries and mortuaries, the trust requirements may differ for each type of Seller.

Surety Bonds

Some states have allowed Sellers to purchase surety bonds to ensure that consumers will get the goods and services they have contracted for rather than requiring the Sellers to put funds in a trust. Not too long ago, there was considerable criticism of Florida law for allowing several multi-state firms to take millions of dollars out of prearrangement trusts by buying surety bonds. Rather than go through the step-by-step logic of why surety bonds aren't good, let me just say that, in my opinion, surety bonds aren't much protection for prearrangement funds.

Cancellations & Changes

It is very important to understand that putting money aside for a Ceremony is not a savings account. The Seller will incur expenses in connection with the prearrangement and, depending upon state law, will be able to recoup all or some of those expenses if you decide to back out of the deal. That being said, many trusts do have provisions for cancellation, although there may be cancellation fees or administrative expenses. That means that you can change your mind in the future and at least get some of the money back.

Note that some trusts cannot be cancelled—that is, they are irrevocable and you cannot get money back. In those cases, funds only are available to provide your Ceremony. The most common reason for setting up trusts as being non-cancelable is to set aside funds for final arrangements and still be able to qualify for certain government benefits.

If you are still paying premiums on an insurance policy and you stop making payments, generally you'll just get a paid-up insurance policy for a lesser amount. Canceling an insurance policy or turning it in for its cash value usually will result in a substantially lower amount received back relative to what was paid in premiums.

Another issue you should consider is what happens if you decide to change your prearrangement. Your prearrangement documents should explain what will happen if you want changes. If you are adding to the goods and services you want for your Ceremony, most Sellers will do everything possible to accommodate that. However, if you are reducing what you want, that may not be as easy. This is because the Financial Tool was set up with certain assumptions by the Seller about how they would recover their selling costs. They incur those costs when the prearrangement is made—a later reduction in the Ceremony doesn't decrease the expenses they already have incurred. It is common to have some sort of fee or penalty charged if there is a reduction in the Ceremony. If the Financial Tool was a non-cancelable trust, it may not be possible to reduce the goods and services to be delivered.

Portability

One of the commonly asked questions when making a prearrangement is "What happens if I move?" Generally, delivery or price guarantees of one Provider will not be honored by another Provider. This is because there are substantial pricing and cost differences between various parts of the country as well as between Providers in some areas.

If you move but still use the Provider specified in your prearrangement, most of the prearrangement will still work for you. There may be some additional charges for transportation, but the specified Provider still will honor its delivery promises. On the other hand, if you move and will not use the specified Provider, you will lose whatever delivery guarantees the Seller and Provider gave you as part of the prearrangement.

If a trust was the Financial Tool, then you may have cancellation fees that will be applied before a refund is made to you. Depending upon state law, these fees may range from nominal to substantial.

With insurance, if you do not use the designated Provider, you still give up the delivery guarantees. However, you do receive the full amount of the policy at the time of death. So, there is no penalty, in terms of lower amount of money received, for not using the specified Provider. Similarly, if your Financial Tool was a bank savings account, you own the account no matter what happens. If it was used as part of a prearrangement, you still lose the delivery guarantee, but you get the full account balance.

From a portability standpoint, insurance policies and bank savings accounts give you the most flexibility. However, whether these two tools are available to you will depend, as in many other cases, on what your state allows in terms of permitted Financial Tools and limits on delivery guarantees that may be made by Sellers and Providers.

Non-Prearrangement Options

Sometimes, people want to set money aside for Ceremonies and final expenses but, for personal reasons, do not want to make an actual prearrangement. This can be done by buying a final expense insurance policy that is not coupled with an agreement to provide goods and services or by putting money in a bank savings account.

Bank savings passbooks can be used to establish a simple pay-on-death trust, often referred to as a Totten Trust. When an account is established, you specify who will be paid from the trust at the time of death. The interest stays in the account and you can change the at-death beneficiary at any time you want or even close the account. It's your money and you stay in control of it, so it's very portable. What you don't get that you get with most insurance and other trust methods of prearranging a funeral is the price guarantee from the mortuary. If you believe that the interest rate on the savings account will match the increases in Ceremony prices, then the price guarantee isn't very important.

Estate Plans & Wills

Although many people think about having a will, it's surprising how many times action is never taken to make or update one. The need for a will differs from state to state. The only thing you can be sure of is that if you need a will and don't have one, the government already has decided how things will be split up! So it's worth a little bit of effort to (1) determine if you need a will and (2) get one drawn up, if necessary. As a generalization, wills are needed when there is real estate owned, when the estate is large enough to be liable for inheritance taxes, or when you want to leave your money and possessions to someone in a manner that is outside of your state's default method of distribution. There are many sources of information to help you determine if you need a will for yourself. Obviously hiring an attorney is common, but there are a number of other sources for general information—local bar associations, books on the subject, state agencies, and Internet sites. Some states allow a simple standard form to be used for straightforward estates.

Still, when you go to the effort of getting a will, it only protects your heirs if you keep it current. If it isn't updated as circumstances change, your assets won't go where you want them to go. No matter what you might say to people, it's a long hard road to overturn the provisions of a written will. Avoid problems—if you need a will, get one and keep it up to date. This is even more important for those with large estates. Congress likes to tinker with tax law, and each change may have an impact on your estate. If you are fortunate enough to have the potential of paying estate taxes, periodically reviewing your will and other estate plans should be on your "must do" list.

Durable Power Of Attorney

A "power of attorney" is a document that allows another person to act for you. The person giving the power is the principal and the person designated to act is called the attorney-in-fact. A Durable Power of Attorney for Health Care is a legal way to express your wishes and gives your Attorney-In-Fact the necessary authority and power to act on your behalf. A Durable Power of Attorney for Health Care is different from a Durable Power of Attorney that allows someone to handle financial affairs for you.

Many of us have fears about what will happen in the event of a long lingering illness. My mother had a fear of becoming a "vegetable," so she executed specific written instructions about what was to happen if she were totally incapacitated. She used a Durable Power of Attorney for Health Care to accomplish this. When properly written and signed, this document specifies who can make decisions about your health care for you when you are unable to make decisions for yourself as well as giving instructions about what sort of efforts should be taken to keep you alive.

A Durable Power of Attorney for Health Care also can be used to specify who can make funeral arrangements for you. State laws set a specific order for people who have the authority to make funeral arrangements. The common order is spouse, children, and then parents. However, a properly drawn Durable Power of Attorney for Health Care can override that. There are a number of reasons for doing this. A common one is practicality. If you have no living or close family members, then this is a way of making sure your final arrangements will be taken care of. Another reason involves relationships where there is not a legal marriage. A Durable Power of Attorney for Health Care is a means of giving a partner the same right to control arrangements as if there were a marriage. Note that state laws differ on the requirements for allowing a Durable Power of Attorney for Health Care to include authority to make funeral arrangements, so make sure any form you sign will allow your attorney-in-fact to function as you expect.

A Durable Power of Attorney for Health Care is a legal document which, to be valid, must conform to your state law. Some hospitals or other organizations have standardized Durable Powers of Attorney for Health Care forms that take care of this. Your physician is also a source for information—although doctors can't give you legal advice, they do know which forms of Durable Power of Attorney they are willing to follow.

Some states have adopted standardized forms; in other cases, it's necessary to have a lawyer draft the document. Power of Attorney forms are available on the Internet, but you should make sure that a given form follows your state's legal requirements. The best way to ensure the effectiveness of a form is to have it drafted by an attorney. Because these are relatively routine documents, drafting by a qualified attorney should not be very expensive.

Power of Attorney forms must be signed and witnessed. In some instances, notarization also is required.

Organ Donations

A lot has been written promoting organ donations. Many states have procedures making it easy to donate organs, even including instructions on driver's licenses. The decision to give part of your body to help someone else is very personal. Most standard forms for organ donation allow specifying which organs may be used or provide a check box for allowing use or transplant of anything that will help another person.

As one with a fear of hospitals, needles, and most things medical, I can understand why people might be reluctant to have themselves "cut up and distributed" after death. Conversely, it won't hurt and may save, prolong, or improve the life of another human being. What a wonderful legacy! ✳

9. Where To Buy?

Choosing a mortuary or cemetery is an important decision. If prearrangements are being made, the decision is difficult enough. But if the decision is being made when a death occurs, then it's even more challenging.

Over the last decade, there has been a lot of consolidation in the ownership of cemeteries and mortuaries. The largest publicly traded cemetery and mortuary consolidation companies have maintained a business model of buying mortuaries and cemeteries with good local reputations and not changing their names. In many cases, the former owners are kept on as employees or consultants. This has the effect of making a mortuary or cemetery owned by a large chain look like it still are locally owned and managed.

While there is nothing inherently wrong about being big or owning many cemeteries or mortuaries, don't take it for granted that you are dealing with independent firms, particularly when doing price comparisons. One woman in Florida reported that she had tried to be a conscientious consumer and compare the prices of three different mortuaries. She was quite upset when she found out that the same publicly traded company owned all three. It's entirely proper to ask a mortuary or cemetery about ownership. If they're reluctant to discuss the subject, perhaps they find the ownership connection embarrassing. Regardless of the answer, how forthcoming they are with information may tell you something about how they view consumers.

There are four basic items to consider when choosing a mortuary or cemetery: price, services, facilities, and location. Each family needs to determine its own priority ranking of these items.

Many of the articles and books about funerals focus primarily on price. However, to some degree, price is important relative to what you get. You expect to pay more for a Cadillac than for a Chevy, even though both do the same thing. How much more you are willing to pay for the luxury car is a value judgment.

While price is always important, you also need to evaluate what you get for what you pay. This is a little different from the concept of getting what you pay for—you should always get what you pay for. However, the value you place on what you get is subjective. Everyone's spending decisions are influenced by how much they value the thing or services they are buying. For example, one consumer may be unwilling to pay anything extra for a zillion watt sound system in a new car. Another person might be willing to buy the car just because of the teeth-rattling sound system. Each view is valid, but the different conclusions reflect different perceived values. Relating this to buying Ceremonies, one consumer may put a high value on the quality of a mortuary's chapel while another might put a low value on it because they intend to use their own church for the Ceremony.

Mortuaries

Should you choose a small neighborhood mortuary (funeral home)? A mortuary chain? A mortuary in a cemetery? Do you just go where you went before?

The best way to choose a mortuary is to shop and compare when you don't have pressure to make a decision. Look at the facilities. Ask others about their experiences. If you are unable to visit in person, call them on the telephone to check prices and discuss their services. Ask them to mail their General Price List and Casket Price List to you or look for pricing information on their Internet site—the more progressive mortuaries will make it easy for you to get information.

If you know people who have lost someone close to them, ask them about their experience. I recently talked to a friend who had experienced deaths of two relatives in the past year. For his mother, the family had used a long established local mortuary. But when his wife's mother passed away almost a year later, they used another mortuary. As he described it, there was a big difference in the level of service, staff attentiveness, and attention to detail. The mortuary that the family felt gave superior service was actually less expensive. So if you have time, do ask others about their experiences. If you are a member of a church, you may find that your clergyperson has experienced the service levels of various mortuaries first hand.

Neighborhood mortuaries may have the advantage of convenience. However, maintaining a complete mortuary is costly, and unless they serve many families each week, their prices may be more expensive than those of larger mortuaries. It is simply a question of overhead being covered by more Ceremonies. In most areas, mortuary prices vary substantially. Often preconceptions based on looking at a facility—"it looks so beautiful, it must be expensive"—are often wrong.

Mortuaries located within cemetery grounds allow you to make all your arrangements in one visit. Many of these mortuaries also have churches or chapels on the premises, eliminating the need for a procession over city streets or freeways. Additionally, these mortuaries have a theoretical advantage of spreading their overhead over more services and that may result in lower prices.

Professional Services

States treat mortuaries and funeral directors as professions that require licensing. In many states, the funeral director's license allows the funeral director to operate a funeral establishment and perform embalming. California separates the funeral director's license from the licensing of embalmers. The former allows an individual to manage a mortuary, while the latter permits a person to do embalming and other preparation of the deceased.

There are also philosophical differences among states in licensing firms versus individuals. Some states have laws that require the funeral director's name to be the name of the establishment. Some do not allow anyone but a licensed funeral director to own a mortuary.[1]

There are two basic reasons for licensing mortuaries. First, the care of the dead has public health implications that are a fundamental responsibility of government. Second, there is a concern about protecting grieving consumers from unscrupulous practices and misrepresentations.

Comparing Mortuaries

One of the most common (and most obvious) ways to compare mortuaries is by price. The downside to this is that it isn't always easy. The United States Federal Trade Commission (FTC) adopted a Funeral Rule in 1982 that mandated price disclosures (see Chapter Twelve for more on this). However, each mortuary puts this information in a slightly different form. Appendix B is a list of goods and services you might purchase from cemeteries and mortuaries to help you compare prices. It includes a lot of detail that may seem unnecessary, but the reason for inclusion is to allow you to make an "apples to apples" comparison. Just like buying a car, you want to make sure that you know what items are included and what are not. If you're not certain about whether an item is included or not, ask. If you don't get a straightforward, understandable answer, worry.

Price is important, but it isn't everything. You can get a hotel room for under $50, but the quality of its amenities won't match that of what you'd get at a five-star resort. The same is true for mortuaries.

Although price comparisons are a good idea, comparisons are not always easy to do. Although the FTC does mandate certain price disclosures, many mortuaries offer more options than are included in the mandated FTC General Price List. As consumers have looked for more ways to personalize a Ceremony, the offerings by mortuaries have increased dramatically. Realizing that more choices made things even more confusing, the mortuaries began to offer packages that consisted of bundles of goods and services as an alternative to buying "a la carte."

Because each firm has its own ideas about what makes a good package, comparing packages can be difficult. How do you deal with this? If you don't want to face the details involved in building your own Ceremony piece by piece from the comprehensive offerings, just compare packages that have the things you want and figure anything else included is just being thrown in. This is somewhat like buying a car off the lot—you accept it with whatever options are already installed. Do discuss prices with the mortuary. This will help you understand what their services are, but more importantly, you'll also get a sense of how consumer oriented they are through that discussion.

Quality of facilities and staff varies greatly. Look at the mortuaries that interest you. How well are the buildings maintained? Do you like the atmosphere? Most importantly, is the staff helpful? Do they seem to care? Do you find them well informed and flexible? These last points are essential to consider when you want to be able to do things your way. A staff that cares about your needs and wishes is much more likely to help you get the type of Ceremony, cremation, or burial you want, whether it be simple or elaborate.

Small firms will have a different approach from larger firms. This isn't good or bad; it's just different. According to the National Funeral Directors Association, its average member performs 187 funerals per year.[2] That means it's likely that one member of the staff will make the Ceremony arrangements and direct the service. After all, they have the time. It also means that on 40 percent of the days of operation (assuming they hold Ceremonies six days per week) their facility will not have a Ceremony. Thus the overhead for the building, autos, personnel, and so on must be recovered from a relatively small number of services.

The staff of a larger firm is more likely to be somewhat specialized. They'll have different people performing various functions based on the belief that the staff can better serve by being intensively trained in specific areas such as helping families to make arrangements when death occurs, embalming, conducting the service, and making prearrangements. This is efficient and may lead to lower prices.

Many people choose a mortuary because they've used the establishment before. While that is a good starting place, the earlier description of how the big chains buy smaller firms and don't change the name suggests that some inquiries may be called for. Although the same name is over the door, it may have new owners—even if the same person appears to be running it. Remember, there is nothing wrong with asking.

Cemeteries

Cemeteries come in many shapes, sizes, and forms of organization. A traditional cemetery has ground burials and above ground memorials (also known as tombstones, monuments, or markers). A memorial-park type of cemetery doesn't have upright monuments. Instead, it has memorials that are flush with the grass to create a more open feeling. There are cemeteries that have "memorial-park" in their names, but still use upright monuments.

Most cemeteries have a number of options for burial.

First, there is ground burial. This is very traditional and often what people think of in relation to a cemetery. An outer burial container is used in conjunction with these burial locations. An outer burial container is an enclosure, usually made of concrete, that helps protect the casket and prevents the ground from collapsing (*See* Figure 17, page 146).

Second, there are lawn crypts. While similar to ground burial, no outer burial container is used because a concrete struc-

Figure 5. Traditional cemeteries have at least some upright monuments. This particular traditional section has a mix of monuments and flush memorials.

Figure 6. A memorial-park style cemetery is characterized by open vistas and sweeping lawns made possible by flush memorials.

Figure 7. Companion lawn crypts under construction

ture to hold the caskets is installed in a large area as part of the development. Lawn crypts are most commonly found as single or companion crypts. The latter have space for two burials, one above the other (see Figures 8 and 9).

Third, there is the broad classification of above ground burial. The most common form is the community mausoleum—crypts built above ground with marble or granite fronts where the name of the deceased and other information is placed. Whereas a mausoleum generally has the crypts located indoors, a garden mausoleum, sometimes called wall crypts, has outdoor crypts. There are also individual, private mausoleums. These can have space for multiple burials and might include a dozen or more crypts. These private mausoleums can be quite expensive. In some areas, owning a family mausoleum is a mark of community status as well as wealth.

Cemeteries can be operated by for-profit, not-for-profit, or government organizations. Churches, mutual benefit associations, or fraternal orders can operate not-for-profit cemeteries. Generally, church owned cemeteries are not covered by the same legal requirements that apply to other private cemeteries. For example, in California religious cemeteries are not required to have endowment care funds or to license their sales staff.

Figure 8. Cross section of companion lawn crypt. (Not to scale, conceptual drawing only, construction details vary.)

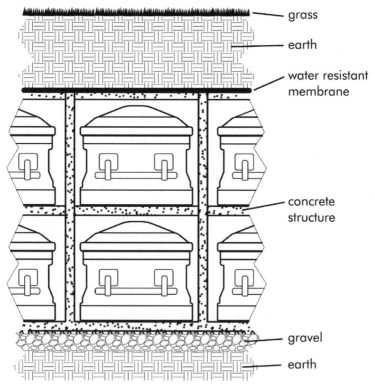

Comparing Cemeteries

To compare cemeteries, consider the condition of the cemetery now, the condition of the cemetery in the future, services offered, and the trust you have in the cemetery organization.

To determine the condition of the cemetery, drive through it and see how well the grounds are cared for. Is the grass well maintained? Has trash been picked up? What is the condition of the buildings? Have trees and shrubs been maintained well? Get out of your car and actually walk into a section or two and see what the condition is. Highly visible, frequently visited areas may get more attention than older, less visible areas. Are the areas that seem to be sold out as well maintained as the areas that are currently on sale? Once you get away from the road and away from areas that are currently for sale, you should get an accurate sense of the level of care and attention given to grounds maintenance.

Figure 9. Cross section of single lawn crypt. (Not to scale, conceptual drawing only, construction details vary.)

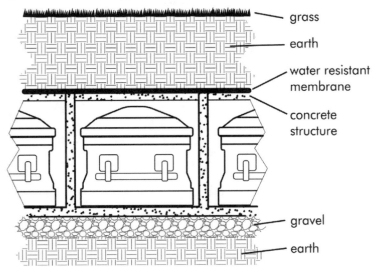

grass

earth

water resistant membrane

concrete structure

gravel

earth

The current condition of the grounds is an indication of future care. If the grounds are being well cared for now, is there a reason why you expect that to change in the future? Current care, though, is not the whole story. Most cemeteries that are not substantially sold out subsidize maintenance from current operating revenues. Ultimately, a cemetery will depend upon its endowment care fund to provide funds for maintenance and upkeep.

What Is An Endowment Care Fund?

Many states require cemeteries to set aside funds for the future care of the cemetery. These funds used to be called perpetual care funds, but the trend has been to call them endowment care funds. The reason for requiring these funds is that cemeteries have a finite economic life. Once all of the burial spaces are sold and the last burial is made, there is no further income to take care of the cemetery—mow the grass, maintain roads, and so on.

Although states may require private cemeteries to have endowment care funds, religious and government owned cemeteries are usually exempt from the requirement.

States that require

Figure 10. An indoor mausoleum.

124

Figure 11. A private mausoleum built in the 1930s for one family.

endowment care funds also adopt laws and regulations governing the investment and use of the funds. The most common restriction is that only the income from the funds can be used for the care and upkeep of the cemetery. Also, there are often restrictions on investments. The state agencies that are responsible for monitoring and regulating cemetery endowment care funds may be located almost any place in state government. Examples of places in state government charged with this responsibility are: Department of Banking, Department of Insurance, Department of Consumer Affairs, Attorney General, or Real Estate Commissioner.

Whether legally required or not, eventually the income from the endowment care fund will be the only source of funds for maintenance of a cemetery. No one can honestly promise how big the endowment care fund will be in the future, when the cemetery is sold out. However, there are current factors that give some indication of what the future may hold. How big is the fund now? How much is added to the fund from each purchase?

Unless you're into financial calculations, the size of the fund may be hard to put into perspective, so let me explain a little of the usual mechanics about how these funds operate. Endowment care funds generally have their principal or corpus protected by law. Cemeteries only are allowed to use the income generated by the fund—interest and dividends—for maintenance. So suppose you have a sold-out twenty-acre cemetery with a $1 million endowment care fund. To most of us, a million dollars seems like a lot of money. Let's see how much care can be provided with that $1 million:

> At a rate of 5 percent for income from dividends and interest, that fund would produce $50,000 a year in income.[3] Sounds okay, so far. That works out to be about $2,500 per acre per year or $208.33 a month. If the cemetery has 1,000 burials per acre that would be $2.50 per year per burial space—just $0.21 per month per space. So here's the question: Do you think the cemetery can take care of mowing the grass, trimming around memorials, trimming trees and shrubs, raking up leaves, watering (if necessary), repairing roads, maintaining walls and walkways, and whatever else is necessary for that amount of money? What are your expectations about the level of care you want in the future if you or your relatives are to be buried in that cemetery?

The amount of money currently in an endowment care fund and the amount added from each sale have a direct impact on what the future of the cemetery will be like.

Let me give you a real world example. In the early 1990s, the

California Department of Consumer Affairs was unhappy that an independent cemetery board rather than a bureau within the department regulated cemeteries.[4] In a workshop on the subject in San Diego, Jim Conran, then head of the department, said that the Cemetery Board needed more funding because it was responsible for over $400 million in endowment care trust funds. I did a quick calculation in my head and realized that Forest Lawn's endowment care funds were a little more than 20 percent of the funds supervised by the state. However, Forest Lawn only had four of the two hundred cemetery licenses in the state. So what did that say about most cemeteries' endowment care funds? I also should mention that about four years after that we decided that even though we had greatly exceeded legal requirements for additions to the funds, we did not think our funds would allow the high quality of maintenance that we wanted. Consequently, we made a substantial increase in the amount put in the endowment care fund from each sale.

At the risk of being accused of bragging about Forest Lawn (although I am), here is a more recent example. Forest Lawn's chief financial officer recently pored through government filings for one of the publicly traded funeral and cemetery corporations. From the documents, he was able to determine the total acreage of its cemeteries and the total amount in its endowment care funds. It came out to about $18,000 per acre. When he did the same calculation for Forest Lawn's cemeteries, he determined it was about $187,000 per acre. Now, there are many possible reasons for differences—amount of land developed, age of the cemetery, permitted investments, amount of additions to the fund, and so on For example, a large cemetery that is relatively new will have sold little land compared to a more mature property and would be expected to have a small fund. A better comparison could be made by looking at the amount of endowment care funds per developed acre. However, even that isn't a perfect comparison because cemeteries not only vary in size, they also vary in costs of maintenance. Such things as what structures are on the property, weather, and labor costs influence the cost of maintenance.

It is sad, but many cemeteries have not put enough money in their endowment care funds to maintain the cemetery when it is sold out. Accordingly, asking about the size of an endowment care fund for a cemetery where you are considering buying burial property is really asking about the future of the cemetery. The answers you get to questions about endowment care funds also may tell you something about the philosophy of those responsible for operating the cemetery. In the United States, cemeteries are expected to be around for a very long time, if not forever. A cemetery management that understands the awesome responsibility it has for the future usually will be equally concerned about the present.

Memorial Societies

Memorial societies are on the fringe of the funeral profession. Usually they are not-for-profit entities that define themselves as being some sort of consumer advocate, as they tend to focus on price rather than value. Many of these organizations provide good information about the funeral process. However, most also have a bias against the rest of the profession—particularly against traditional mortuaries and cemeteries.

Memorial societies usually do not view themselves as being part of the funeral profession. Nevertheless, as they give advice about funeral arrangements, it seems fair to classify them as being a part of the industry. In general, memorial societies give advice and do not (often cannot) sell funeral goods and services. Some memorial societies enter into arrangements with local mortuaries or third party sellers to get discounted services for their members. Only a little shopping will determine if the discounted price is really a good deal or not.

Cremation Societies

As for cremation societies, each of the publicly traded, for-profit companies operates one or more subsidiaries selling cremations and uses the word "society" in the subsidiary's name. So the word "society" doesn't mean that the organization is not-for-profit. There is nothing wrong with operating an organization with the intent to make a profit. Just don't assume that there isn't a profit motive because of the word "society" in a name.

Most cremation societies are oriented primarily toward performing no-frills, "practical" dispositions. On the coasts, this most often would be a cremation with no service and the cremated remains scattered at sea. Some societies quote some very low prices. These may be legitimate, as cremation societies may have substantially lower overhead than mortuaries. However, the prices may not be all-inclusive and may be designed just to get consumers "in the door."

See Chapter 6 for more information about cremations.

Monument Dealers

Monument dealers, sometimes known as monument builders or memorial dealers, sell various types of products to identify burial locations. The term "monument" is something of a misnomer. The term invokes visions of large granite objects with names and dates chiseled into their faces. However, the items monument dealers usually sell are more correctly described under the more generic term of "memorials." Memorials include the classic upright monuments sometimes called tombstones as well as flush memorials of bronze or granite. The latter are sometimes referred to as markers or memorial tablets. A monument dealer primarily sells memorials of various types, yet also may sell other burial related merchandise. Monument dealers often will do the final inscriptions or artwork on granite memorials but usually will contract with a foundry for production of bronze memorials.

Many of the products sold by monument dealers also are available through mortuaries and cemeteries, unless prohibited by state laws.

A cemetery cannot require you to purchase a memorial from it, but it may set rules and regulations about size, material, and installation method. These rules must apply to the cemetery itself as well as any memorials brought in from other sellers. Also, a cemetery may refuse to allow a memorial that does not conform to its specifications. If you consider buying a memorial from a seller other than the cemetery, it would be a good idea to contact the cemetery for its specifications and rules before making a purchase.[5] See "Memorials, Monuments, & Markers" on page 147.

Retail Casket Sellers

Traditionally, only mortuaries sold caskets. In the last decade, however, there has been a growth in non-mortuary sales of caskets—usually by storefront retail casket stores.

The casket stores have promoted their merchandise by decrying the markups mortuaries have made on caskets. Historically, mortuaries have, indeed, recovered a substantial portion of their overhead from caskets. However, as the mortuaries increasingly lost sales to the casket stores, they began to adjust their prices to reflect the new competition. In general, they increased service prices and decreased their casket prices. Some mortuaries have offered substantial discounts on packages that include services, caskets, and other goods.

As suggested throughout this book, price-conscious consumers should comparison shop. The casket stores want to be thought of as discount stores, but that isn't always the case. The only way to find out for sure is to do the homework. The most difficult part of comparison-shopping for caskets is to make sure that you are comparing like merchandise. In the case of caskets manufactured by the large, national companies—Batesville Casket Company and Aurora Casket Company—it's relatively easy. However, there are a number of smaller high-quality manufacturers also. Therefore, be sure to take careful notes about quality of construction, material, gauge (thickness) of metal caskets, type of fabric, ornamentation, and finish. The goal is to get what you want at a price you feel is reasonable.

Price Comparisons

In a recent focus group, we asked consumers if pricing was an important element in making a decision about a mortuary. It wasn't surprising that there was general agreement that cost was important. Nonetheless, we know from decades of experience that few consumers actually price shop mortuaries or cemeteries. True, more do now than ever, but it's still a small percentage. Even among the members of the focus group, few of those who actually had made funeral arrangements did price comparison-shopping. In theory, comparing prices should be easy since mortuaries must give out price information. If you stop by a mortuary to inquire about prices, the mortuary is required to give you a copy of its General Price List before discussing arrangements. Most mortuaries and cemeteries are more than willing to give full pricing information over the phone. If they aren't, I'd be concerned about doing business with them—unwillingness to give out price information shows a lack of respect for consumers.

Although cemeteries are not covered by the FTC's Funeral Rule requirements on price disclosures, most cemeteries are more than willing to quote prices in person or over the phone. Still, there are exceptions. For instance, a local church-owned cemetery in Los Angeles has a policy not to quote prices over the phone. Personally, I don't think that shows much respect for consumers, and I'm not comfortable dealing with organizations that are not forthcoming with information about prices and policies.

The challenge in making price comparisons is to make sure that you are comparing "apples to apples"—that the same items are included in each case. As more and more options are offered, the pricing gets more complicated. From a business standpoint, I know that some of Forest Lawn's competitors will respond to a question like "What is a funeral going to cost?" with a quote of the firm's basic services charge.[6] However, a number of things aren't included in the basic charge: caskets, flowers, limousines, casket (pall) bearers, outer burial containers, and so on. To paraphrase an old adage, if the price seems too low to be believable, it probably isn't believable.

The point is that you must be meticulous in your questions about what is included and what is not included when you are comparing prices. To help do this, Appendix B includes a list of items most commonly purchased as part of a traditional Ceremony and burial. Even if the price comparison is difficult, you may find that you are more comfortable with one mortuary over another in the way they help you understand what they offer and how it's priced. Most organizations have learned that prices are just one factor that consumers use to make decisions. The majority of consumers make decisions on total perceived value, which is a combination of price, quality, and overall satisfaction.

Do It Yourself

Some have suggested that you don't really need a funeral director or mortuary to handle the details. In other words, you can "do it yourself." It's true that many things can be done directly by a family to bypass the services of a mortuary. These include obtaining and filing the death certificate, getting a burial permit, buying a casket and outer burial container (often required by a cemetery), holding a Ceremony or viewing in your home rather than a church or mortuary chapel, and transporting the deceased to the cemetery or crematory. The literature on this suggests that doing all or some of these things yourself saves money, keeps you out of the clutches of the local mortuary, and helps your grieving process by being intimately involved in the process of final arrangements.

Of course, consumers cannot do some things for themselves. Only people who have specific types of licenses can perform some activities. Generally, licensing is based upon requirements for specialized training or examinations to demonstrate skill and knowledge. On the mortuary side, all states allow only licensed funeral directors or embalmers to embalm a body (see Chapter 11 for information about embalming). Subject to individual state law, only coroners, medical examiners, or licensed physicians can sign death certificates, although once the proper signature is obtained, anyone can file the document.

For most people, the ability to do these things is largely theoretical. Most families don't want to cope with the details or bureaucracy needed to do everything themselves. Although there is a potential cost savings, American society is conditioned to hiring others to perform service work. Fewer and fewer people repair their cars or appliances. We either throw something away and buy another or find someone else to do the repairs. When it comes to dealing with the death of someone they love, most people would rather focus on what is going to be done to say goodbye in a meaningful way rather than manage the mechanics of getting it accomplished. One of the reasons people turn to mortuaries is that they want someone else to handle all the details. When overwhelmed by grief, it can be hard to make decisions as well as organize and do the follow-through necessary for a Ceremony.

However, it's possible to control expense and still not have to do everything yourself. The best way, of course, is to make your plans before death occurs. I keep stressing this because I believe in it. Having discussions with your spouse and family members doesn't cost you anything. The reward of just putting your wishes in writing is tremendous peace of mind. The decision to prearrange by financing a future Ceremony is an independent but vitally important decision. Prearrangement is discussed in Chapters 7 and 8. 🍁

10. What Do I Need To Buy?

Once you have determined whom you want to buy from, the next issue is what to buy. Given the variation between what different mortuaries offer, the purchase possibilities seem almost endless. So this chapter only will discuss buying caskets, burial property, outer burial containers, and memorials/monuments.

Caskets

Caskets are available in many colors, features, types of construction, and adornments. Simple cloth covered wooden caskets are the least expensive, while the most expensive caskets are made of bronze. In between are caskets made of steel of varying thickness, copper, redwood, and hardwoods (maple, oak, etc.). They also are manufactured in many colors and designs.

Most caskets are made of wood or metal. Although there have been some caskets made from plastic or fiberglass available from time to time, they still are not seen often. Some wooden caskets are covered with cloth. Some metal caskets have "sealing" features, including gaskets intended to keep out water, air, and underground life. Almost all caskets are fabric lined, but many different types and colors of fabric are used. In fact, there are other differences, some of which are more obvious than others.

The wood used in cloth-covered caskets is usually a soft wood, often a pressboard type of material. As the pressboard itself is rather unattractive, it's covered with cloth to improve the appearance of the casket.

Wooden caskets can be made from relatively soft woods like pine or poplar, hardwoods like oak or walnut, or exotic woods like mahogany.

Metal caskets are made from several different materials: steel, stainless steel, copper, and bronze. Steel is rated by its thickness that is measured by gauge. It's important to understand that the lower the number the thicker the steel; higher numbers mean thinner steel. Thus, a casket made of 20-gauge steel has thinner metal than a casket made of 16-gauge steel.

Although technically not caskets, most mortuaries have "alternative containers" available for cremation. The alternative containers may be made of cardboard, pressed wood, or canvas. Most mortuaries will carry only one type of alternative container. Furthermore, they usually have policies preventing having a deceased in an alternative container from being present at a Ceremony. This is because the alternative containers are generally much more difficult for them to handle than a casket.

As mentioned before, mortuaries historically recovered a large part of their overhead in the markup from the wholesale casket cost. The entry of retail casket stores as competitors has tended to push down the prices of caskets and raise the prices of mortuary services. As a result, although the mortuaries are required to make the goods and services available individually, some have begun to offer attractively priced packages that include caskets—effectively lowering the casket price.[1]

As advocated throughout this book, never hesitate to comparison shop, but also make sure you are looking at the total rather than just one or two components. That way you'll know whether or not you are better off buying from several sources or a single source. Undoubtedly, the best way to avoid emotional overspending is to discuss Ceremony options and caskets ahead of time. Ceremonies are discussed in Chapter 5 and prearrangement purchases are discussed in Chapter 8.

Choosing A Casket

The choice of casket is very subjective and a matter of personal taste as well as price. Design, material, color, features, and price all play a part in the decision. Some consumer organizations have criticized those buying or selling expensive caskets—"they all do the same thing." Yet this decision is like many other decisions consumers make. A low cost car fulfills the same basic transportation need that a big sports utility vehicle or luxury car does, but most consumers don't buy the

Figure 12. An inexpensive, cloth covered casket. *Photo from Forest Lawn Mortuary.*

lowest cost vehicle or the most expensive vehicle. Similarly, there are wide price variations in furniture prices. Consumers buy what fits into their budgets and appeals to their sense of value and aesthetics.

Similarly, there isn't a right or wrong in choosing a casket. Decide what you like and compare prices. Find out if you save money by buying a casket in one place and funeral services at another. Some mortuaries have begun to implement aggressive package pricing plans that substantially offset the advantages of buying a casket from a casket store. But you never know until you check it out. There is also the subjective value that you may place on convenience—everything in one place versus cost savings on one item purchased. Sometimes you can have it all; you just need to make the effort to find out what is available.

Figure 13. An example of a premium metal casket. *Photo from Forest Lawn Mortuary.*

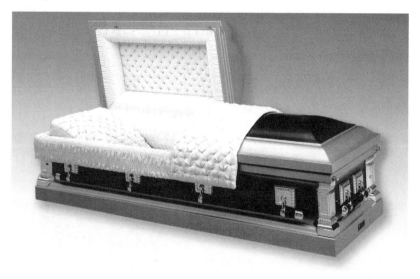

Rental Caskets

Some mortuaries offer rental caskets. What is "rented" is a nice outer shell that has an inexpensive insert placed inside it that actually holds the deceased. The outer shells are made of the same types of materials that most regular caskets are made of—wood or metal. The insert is actually the casket. This is important because many states prohibit the re-use of caskets.

Rental caskets seem to have greater popularity in areas with high cremation rates, as the inserts are made of materials that are appropriate for cremation. This is probably because a metal casket cannot be cremated and some people are reluctant to cremate a higher priced wood casket. A metal or high-quality wood rental casket gives the appearance of a more expensive casket.

Rental caskets also may be used for various forms of burial as long as the insert meets your cemetery's requirements. However, not all mortuaries offer rental caskets. The popularity of rental caskets seems to vary by regions.

Sources And Prices

Caskets have received a lot of attention in recent years, because there are now many sources from which to purchase them: mortuaries, cemeteries, the Internet, and specialized retail stores. The sale of caskets by nontraditional outlets—read that as anyone other than a mortuary—has sparked some controversy. Many funeral directors have maintained that only someone licensed to render at-need professional care should be allowed to sell funeral merchandise such as caskets. Others have believed that consumers would benefit from the competition that should result from having more sellers. State laws run both ways on this.

California allows anyone to sell caskets, but legislatures in Tennessee and Oklahoma passed state laws prohibiting anyone but a licensed funeral director from selling caskets. In 2002, a U.S. Court of Appeals decision struck down the Tennessee law as unconstitutional, while in the same year a lower federal district court upheld the similar Oklahoma law. Obviously, as shown by these two court cases, this is in a state of flux!

Funeral directors have taken the seemingly reasonable position that all sellers of a particular type of merchandise should be under the same rules. For example, California requires that any funeral director who sells a casket preneed put 100 percent of the sales price into a government supervised trust. The California Department of Consumer Affairs opposed legislation that would have put the same trusting requirements on retail stores that sell caskets. That doesn't make much sense. Presumably, the trust is required as security for having the casket delivered when needed, so it's hard to see the logic of not protecting the consumer in the same way with every preneed casket sale. In other states, funeral directors have lobbied for laws restricting sales of caskets to only licensed funeral directors.

With the changes in who sells caskets, there also have been shifts in pricing. Consumers who are most concerned about cost will want to shop at several sources before deciding where to buy. Others will want convenience and are more likely to purchase from the mortuary.

Special Caskets

Caskets for adults generally come in standard sizes. However, there are some instances when a standard-sized casket cannot be used. The most common situation requiring a special casket is due to the size of the deceased. Although most mortuaries usually will not have these in inventory, they typically can obtain an oversize casket within a day or so. Note that oversize caskets may present a problem with the cemetery space size as well.

If you are not dealing with a mortuary that is part of the cemetery, be sure the mortuary tells the cemetery that the casket is oversized, and find out if there are any resulting restrictions or problems. It's the mortuary's responsibility to provide the cemetery with information about the size of the casket if there is anything unusual about its dimensions. The cemetery then can verify whether a given casket will fit in the vault or crypt. If the burial will be in the ground and the vault (outer burial container) is purchased from the mortuary, then the mortuary should check with the cemetery to make sure that the vault will fit in the burial space. If the casket or vault is purchased from a retail store, make sure the store has verified with the cemetery that the sizes of the casket and vault are acceptable. Otherwise, get the dimensions and talk to the cemetery yourself.

Although this may seem to be unnecessary, cemeteries vary greatly in what they consider "standard" sizes of burial spaces. Often there is variation within a single cemetery as well as among cemeteries. The variations have to do with types of construction, changing views of appropriate land use, and historical traditions.

Cemetery Property

The first step in choosing cemetery property, of course, is to choose a cemetery. Next, choose the type of cemetery property you want, and then choose the property based upon location, price, and other features.

Three things usually govern the choice of a cemetery: religious affiliation, prior family use, and location. Some religions expect or require participants to be buried in a cemetery dedicated to that denomination. For example, in some parts of the country the Catholic Church operates cemeteries where a priest has blessed the ground. Often dioceses that have their own cemeteries do not want priests to consecrate ground in non-Catholic cemeteries. Similarly, Jewish law requires the faithful to be buried in a cemetery that is exclusively for Jews. If you are a member of a church and have any question about your faith's doctrine regarding burial, be sure to talk to your clergyperson. If you do not have a religious affiliation that has specific requirements, then you can choose a cemetery based solely upon location or prior family use.

It's useful to know that there are fundamentally two types of cemeteries—traditional cemeteries and memorial-parks. The simple distinction between the two is that traditional cemeteries have upright monuments (tombstones) and memorial-parks do not. However, some traditional cemeteries will have a section with flat memorials that are flush with the ground. The memorial-park is noted especially for its open vistas of sweeping lawns as contrasted with rows of upright monuments in a traditional cemetery (see Figures 5 and 6 on page 120).

If your family has relatives buried in a local cemetery, it probably will be the first one you will consider. If not, then for convenience most people will start by looking at a cemetery near where they live. It isn't too hard to evaluate a cemetery. Drive through it and see what condition it's in. Go to an older area, get out of the car and walk into the section. Note the condition of the grass and the condition of the landscaping. Also, check out a newer area. Is the maintenance similar, or does the cemetery obviously spend a lot more effort on what they are trying to sell.[?] Talk to people at the cemetery. Do you feel they are forthright in answering your questions or are they only interested in selling you something?

In many states, you can inquire with the cemetery licensing authority about the status of the cemetery's license. Note that this isn't always helpful because most states do not license all cemeteries. For example, in California it's believed that there are more than a thousand active cemeteries, but the Department of Consumer Affairs licenses only two hundred of them. The difference lies with the fact that some cemeteries operated by religious organizations and cemetery districts (government) are exempt from most of the regulations that apply to private cemeteries.

Nonetheless, most cemeteries have many different types of

Figure 14. Garden mausoleum (wall crypts) under construction.

burial property. The most common are ground property (graves), lawn crypts, mausoleum crypts, and columbarium niches.

Ground property and lawn crypts are similar in that they look very much the same on the surface—each looks like an area covered with grass. However, with ground property, most cemeteries will require that an outer burial container be used for a burial. Lawn crypt sections have crypt structures that are installed at the time the section is developed (in contrast to being placed at the time of burial), so no outer burial container is necessary. Lawn crypts are often available in single and companion (one above the other) capacities.

Usually, mausoleums are structures for above ground burial.[2] A community mausoleum has many crypts that are sold to many different families. A private mausoleum is built for just one family

Figure 15. A garden mausoleum (wall crypt) development.

Figure 16. An outdoor columbarium with niches for urns containing cremated remains.

and is very expensive. Most mausoleums are finished with attractive marble or granite stonework. If an indoor mausoleum, one can take advantage of visiting it in inclement weather without getting wet or standing out in the cold. Outdoor mausoleums also may be called garden mausoleums or wall crypts. The second and third rows of crypts—often known as the heart and eye levels—are the most expensive.

A columbarium contains niches for placement of cremated remains. Columbaria may be built indoors as part of a mausoleum or freestanding outdoors. A columbarium niche may be able to accommodate more than one urn containing cremated remains, depending upon the size of the niche itself and that of the urns used. Urns are available in a wide variety of sizes.

This discussion of cemetery property covers the variety of options in the simplest of terms. In actuality, most cemeteries have a significant variety of options for burial, from the simple to the very elaborate. In addition to the previously mentioned private mausoleums, there are often many other options for family memorials.

Outer Burial Containers

Outer burial containers are also known as burial vaults, grave liners, or other similar terms. Most cemeteries do require one to help avoid future collapsing of the ground as the casket deteriorates over time. The FTC Funeral Rule prohibits mortuaries from

Figure 17. Cross section of out burial container used for ground burial. (Not to scale, conceptual drawing only, actual construction differs between manufacturers and models.)

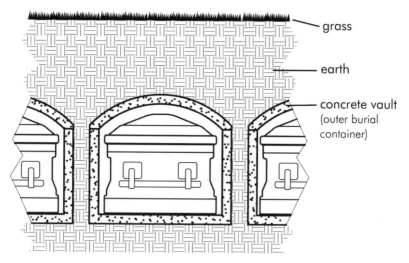

grass

earth

concrete vault (outer burial container)

Figure 18. A simple outer burial conatiner or vault. Note that many different types are available.

representing that state laws require an outer burial container but does allow cemeteries to have their own rule requiring one.

The vault or liner is placed in the ground at the time of burial, and the casket is placed in it during burial. A "bell liner" is made of reinforced concrete and will cover only the top and sides of the casket. The bottom is open to the ground. A vault is usually more substantial and expensive than a bell liner and surrounds the casket on all sides, including the bottom. Some burial vaults are sold with warranties of protective strength.

The most common material vaults are made from is concrete, which may be left as unfinished concrete or be coated with a variety of materials.

Memorials, Monuments, & Markers

The term "monument" is something of a misnomer. The term invokes visions of large granite objects with names and dates chiseled into their faces. The more correct, generic term is memorial . Memorials include the classic upright monuments sometimes called tombstones as well as flush memorials of bronze or granite. The latter are sometimes referred to as markers or memorial tablets.

While a cemetery cannot require that a memorial be purchased from it, most cemeteries have rules and regulations that define the specifications of allowable memorials. The cemetery must apply the same rules to the memorials it sells as to those purchased from other sources. The specifications may include restrictions on such things as material, size, and style. Often the specifications will vary by section or type of burial property of the cemetery. The objective, from the cemetery's viewpoint, is to provide some measure of conformity in aesthetics and maintenance.

Memorials typically are made of either bronze or granite. Bronze is a versatile metal that does not rust and it is possible to cast detail into bronze memorials that cannot be cut into granite. Over time, bronze develops a patina, or coloration, which is the result of oxidation. The color will depend upon environmental conditions—air pollution, exposure to weather, or any other chemicals to which it is exposed. In addition to

Figure 19. A typical bronze memorial.

being used for flush memorials, bronze memorials also are used on mausoleum crypts and cremation niches. Granite is available in many colors and is a very hard stone. It is possible to carve granite into a variety of shapes for upright monuments as well as to use it for flush memorials. Inscriptions in granite memorials often are produced by sand blasting techniques. Although sometimes used for memorials, marble is not a preferred material for outdoor memorials because of its relative softness.

Unless state law prohibits, memorials may be purchased from cemeteries, mortuaries, monument dealers, and some casket stores.

Usually, cemeteries are flexible about the wording of inscriptions on memorials. Nonetheless, most reserve the right to reject a memorial due to an inscription that is obscene, racist, or otherwise objectionable. 🍁

Practical Goodbye

Your lost friends are not dead,
but gone before, advanced a
stage or two upon that road
which you must also travel in the
steps they trod.

Aristophanes

11. When Death Occurs

In the immediate moments after a death occurs, as well as in the hours and days following, there is a lot to do—reporting the death, choosing a mortuary, and notifying family and friends, as well as seemingly countless decisions about the Ceremony.

Who to notify

If death does not occur in a hospital, in most areas the first thing to do is to call 911. Depending upon your location, this will bring paramedics, police, or others who can certify that death has occurred. Some people are reluctant to use the 911 emergency number, but it's very appropriate in this instance. Emergency medical personnel are trained to determine if death actually has occurred. In most instances, local law enforcement also is summoned to be sure there are no suspicious circumstances related to the death.

If the patient is under hospice care, then you may want to call the hospice and let them help you notify the proper authorities.

After the 911 call, the next calls will probably be to family members. If there was a prearranged Ceremony, then the decision about which mortuary to use already has been made. Otherwise, a mortuary needs to be selected and contacted.

Others who should be contacted include doctor(s), employer, friends, insurance agents, clubs, and other organizations. Remember that this doesn't all need to be done at once. In fact, the task of notifying people is a good thing to give family members and close friends who want to help in any way they can.

When To Make The Call?

Sometimes people are reluctant to dial 911. While I do not encourage anyone to practice medicine for themselves, here are some factors that may indicate that death has occurred:

* Breathing stops.

* Heartbeat cannot be detected by putting your head on his/her chest or by putting your finger under the ear.

* Shaking or shouting does not arouse them.

* Eyelids remain slightly open.

* Eyes appear fixed on a certain spot.

* The jaw relaxes and the mouth opens slightly.

If you are not expecting death to occur or are not making decisions based upon a valid "do not resuscitate" instruction, do not wait until any of the above occurs. If you are trying to save a life, the paramedics would much rather be called too early than too late. In cases of serious or terminal illnesses, it's best to talk with a physician about what you should do and when.

Decisions To Be Made

Many times, it seems that with the end questions just begin. Although there are many decisions to be made, don't hesitate to pause and proceed only at your own comfort level. The loss of someone you love is emotionally draining and can make decision-making difficult. Use family and friends for help and support.

Which Mortuary To Use?

If you have prearranged, you'll probably have the answer to this question before you need it. That's good, because it means that you were able to make a deliberate, calm decision. If you haven't thought about this or determined ahead of time, then you will need to make a decision quickly. In that case, there are several possible sources for information, including family, friends, and clergy.

Contacting The Mortuary

When contacting a mortuary, you will be asked for some basic information that will allow the mortuary to make the removal:

* Your name and relationship to the deceased.

* The name of the deceased.

* Location of deceased (hospital, home, coroner's office, and so on).

> ✱ How to contact you or the person who will be responsible for making arrangements.

Embalming Or Refrigeration

Until about 1860, bodies usually were packed in ice as soon as they had been bathed. This allowed time for friends and families to gather for the Ceremony. When arterial embalming was developed, refrigeration generally was discontinued as a way to preserve the body. The embalming process provides for temporary preservation until the Ceremony is held and is satisfactory for up to a few weeks depending upon the condition of the deceased and the skill of the embalmer. For many years, almost all mortuaries adopted it as a routine procedure unless specifically asked not to do so.

Now the FTC Funeral Rule and most state laws do not allow embalming to be done without permission. If the body isn't embalmed, it may be refrigerated. Many mortuaries have installed special refrigerators and offer refrigeration as an alternative to embalming. With a few exceptions, you can decide whether the body is to be embalmed or refrigerated. Generally, authorization for embalming can be done by telephone, but the mortuary must speak with a person who has the legal right to make that decision. The choice regarding embalming also can be part of a prearrangement.

Charges for refrigeration may be based on the number of days, so if for any reason the Ceremony, cremation, or burial is delayed, the refrigeration charges might be higher than the cost of embalming. If this is a cost issue for you, be sure to ask your funeral director for the difference in charges for embalming and refrigeration. With embalming, more options for the Ceremony arrangements remain open to you. If members of the family would like to view the deceased, embalming is a virtual necessity. Most mortuaries do not want to dress the deceased, have a viewing, or have a Ceremony with an open casket, unless the body has been embalmed. If the body is to be transported by common carrier across state lines, embalming or use of an airtight metal container is required by law. This can be either a casket on an "airtray," which the casket rests on, or some sort of alternative container that is a combination of airtray and casket. In the case of transporting a body to another country, each country has its own laws that govern shipping methods and required paperwork.

What To Take To The Mortuary

Four things that should be taken to the mortuary are: (1) important papers that affect the Ceremony, cremation, or burial, (2) objects to be used at the Ceremony, (3) clothing, and (4) a photograph of the deceased.

Records that are helpful in making arrangements include armed services discharge papers (form DD-214), which are required to secure veterans benefits; documents about any prearrangements to help plan the Ceremony; and copies of any insurance policies that will be used as the source of funds to pay for a Ceremony.

Objects to be used at the Ceremony or visitation do not necessarily need to be taken to the arrangement conference. However, starting to think about what might be meaningful also will help you create a Ceremony that meets your desires.

Clothing should include outerwear as well as underwear, but, usually, no shoes. Although most of the time the clothing is relatively formal—suit and tie for men, dress for women—that is only a custom rather than a requirement.

If there is to be a viewing, a color photograph of the deceased assists the mortuary's professional staff with cosmetics and hair styling.

Arrangement Conference

Sometimes people arrive at the mortuary to make arrangements and expect the process not to take very long. However, the process of making arrangements usually takes several hours. If you are choosing cemetery property in addition to planning a Ceremony, even more time will be needed. The process will be shortened somewhat by having prearranged the Ceremony, but it still takes time to confirm vital statistics, service times, contact participants, and so on.

Who Has The Right?

Although states differ in who has the authority to control the Ceremony, burial, or cremation of a deceased, in general, it's similar to inheritance laws—spouse, children, and then parents. Nevertheless, it is also possible, in many cases, to override the statutory default with a Durable Power of Attorney for Health Care.

If there is to be a burial and the cemetery property is not held in the name of the deceased, most cemeteries will require signed authorization from whoever does own the cemetery property. Also, because of the irreversible nature of cremation, many crematories want all or a majority of people on the same level of authority to sign the authorization. This would more commonly occur when there is more than one adult child making a cremation arrangement. A state's laws for authorizing a burial may be different from those for authorizing a removal or disinterment. Although it's usually clear who has the right, there are nuances that can add to the complexity of final arrangements. Prearrangement or even just putting your wishes in writing can help avoid some of this. Mortuaries and cemeteries are a good source of information regarding who has authority over the various aspects of a Ceremony, burial, or cremation. Unfortunately, many attorneys deal primarily with estate/inheritance rights and these are not always the same as funeral and cemetery laws.

Autopsy

An autopsy is an examination of a body that is performed to determine the cause of death. Autopsies are not done routinely. When the coroner or medical examiner is involved, there is an increased likelihood that an autopsy will be done to determine the cause of death. However, the decision to perform an autopsy at government expense is at the discretion of the coroner who has a legal responsibility to determine the cause of death when no physician was present or where there are suspicious circumstances.

Some families want an autopsy to be performed so they can be "absolutely certain" about the cause of death. Mortuaries do not do autopsies, but there are private firms that perform them. Most often, this is requested for peace of mind or out of frustration/anger in dealing with the death rather than a necessity. If you feel a strong emotional need to have a private autopsy, you might want to seek the counsel of a friend who isn't caught up in the emotional turmoil of the death to help you make a decision about whether or not it's wise or necessary to spend the money.

Mortuaries have different policies regarding autopsies. Some will charge a fee for the use of their facilities for an autopsy, while others do not want autopsies performed in their facilities at all. In the latter case, the mortuary usually feels that it does not have the proper facilities for autopsies to be conducted.

Death Certificates

Each state requires that a death certificate be obtained before burial or cremation can take place. There are two reasons for this.

The first is to make sure that there has been no foul play. In cases were where a doctor has not been in attendance, as specified by state law, the coroner must approve the death certificate.

The second reason is statistical. To aid in their public health programs, states keep information on mortality rates, causes of death, age, race, and other demographic information. The information is not only useful to government, but when the data is aggregated, it is an aid to medical researchers as they seek illness patterns that may help in their quest for new cures.

A mortuary will complete the death certificate and get the required signatures as part of its normal services. However, it is permissible for an individual to gather the information and file the form. Some of the agencies the forms are filed with are quite picky about how the forms are filled out but always will indicate

Figure 19. Typical information required to complete a death certificate.

Decedent Personal Data

Name—first, middle, last
Date of birth
Age
Sex
Date & time of death
State of birth
Social Security number
Military service
Marital status
Education (years completed)
Race
Usual employer
Occupation
Kind of business
Years in occupation

Spouse and Parent Information

Name of surviving spouse—
    first, middle, last (maiden)
Name of father—first, middle,
    last
Birth state
Name of mother—first,
    middle, last (maiden)
Birth state

Usual Residence

Residence—street, city,
    county, zip
Years in county
State or foreign country

Informant (who supplied the information)

Name, relationship
Mailing address (street, city,
    state, zip)

Place of death

Place of death: street address,
    city, county
Cause of Death
Time interval between onset
    and death
If death reported to coroner
Biopsy or autopsy
Other significant conditions
    contributing to death

Disposition

Date
Place of final disposition

Funeral director and local registrar

Type of disposition(s)
Embalmer ID
Funeral Director ID

Physician's Certification

Physician's name & license
    number
Date first attended decedent
Date last seen alive

why they can't or won't accept one. Often the most difficult part of obtaining the death certificate is getting the doctor to sign it. This is because doctors are not always in their offices and when they are, they tend to be fully occupied with patients.

No matter who files the death certificate, there is certain information that needs to be supplied to complete the form. Typical information required to file a death certificate is shown in Figure 19. Family members usually will supply the information about the deceased to complete the Personal Data, Residence, Informant, and Family Information sections. This information also can be collected and recorded as part of a prearrangement. The funeral director will obtain the other information in the Disposition, Funeral Director, Place of Death, and Physician's Certification sections, as well as securing the signature of the attending physician and completing the information regarding embalming, burial, or cremation.

Delays In Burials

Sometimes a burial cannot take place as quickly as a family might like. The most common delays are caused by governmental requirements. The most common, non-weather related delay is due to problems procuring the death certificate. In colder climates where the ground freezes, there are often long delays before burial can be made.

In most jurisdictions, if a doctor is not in attendance at the time of death, a coroner or medical examiner must review the cause of death before signing a death certificate or allowing release of the deceased to the family. The coroner will exercise independent discretion about autopsies and any other medical tests to be performed. The range of delays depends upon how much investigation is needed and the workload of the coroner. Although coroners generally understand how difficult it can be on the surviving family and friends not to proceed with the Ceremony, they have a legal duty to make sure that the cause of death is known. Understandably, this is to make certain that cases involving foul play or suspicious circumstances are brought to the attention of law enforcement and that there are not any public health issues that may affect more people.

In cases where the coroner does not sign the death certificate, it's up to the attending physician to sign the document. Most of the time, the mortuary will prepare the death certificate and deliver it to the doctor for signature. Some jurisdictions are very rigid about how these forms are filled out, which can necessitate several attempts before the local agency accepts the death certificate for filing. Obviously, the need for multiple attempts is frustrating to the mortuary and the doctor as well as possibly causing a delay in the Ceremony. In cases where a burial permit also is needed, it cannot be obtained until the death certificate has been filed.

Out-Of-Area Deaths

Because we've become so mobile, death might occur while traveling. Here is some basic information that will help in this eventuality.

Embalming usually is required for transportation of a deceased by common carrier or across state lines. In the United States, the Federal Trade Commission prohibits mortuaries from making any misrepresentations about embalming being required.

The local, hometown mortuary generally can help make arrangements. They can make contact with a mortuary located where the death took place and coordinate permits and transportation.

A casket is not always required for transportation. Ask about lower cost "air trays." If you purchased a prearrangement, you want to avoid purchasing items from a mortuary other than the one you made prearrangements with because price guarantees usually only apply to goods and services provided by the organization that made the preneed sale.

When a deceased must be transported between countries, consulate certificates and other forms often will be required. There are significant differences between the requirements of various countries. Your mortuary can advise you of the required documents, costs, and other requirements based upon the destination country.

Moving Remains To Another Cemetery

Sometimes people ask if it's possible to move a deceased to another cemetery. Usually, the reason for this is to have a family memorial—to have the deceased members of a family together in one place. Just as the desirability of this is subjective, so is the question of whether it's right or wrong. Both depend upon the values and desires of the individuals involved.

In other instances, the desire to move a deceased from one cemetery to another stems from a cemetery falling into disrepair or other perceived problems that individuals cannot solve or fix themselves. In these cases, though, there may be particular issues that create obstacles to accomplishing the desired objective. So let's first identify what needs to be done in a "normal" case, and then let's explore the complications that might be encountered.

First, it's helpful to understand the role that each cemetery will play in accomplishing the desired goal. The cemetery from which the remains are to be removed usually will require that it perform the actual disinterment.

To remove (disinter) someone from a cemetery will require the signature of an authorized person. State laws generally specify who has the right to authorize burial (interment) as well as who can authorize the removal (see the section "Who Has the Right?" on page 158). Cemeteries will be very concerned about following the letter of the law when performing disinterments, as they do not want the liability of doing them improperly. Their risk is litigation from people with the legal right to control burial or from a regulatory agency that could fine them or revoke their license. Thus, even though a cemetery manager may empathize with the expressed desire, the cemetery's actions are constrained by forces beyond its control.

After the question of proper authorization is addressed, arrangements can be made with both the cemetery where the removal will take place and the new cemetery. Most cemeteries will not make a removal in another cemetery because they do not want the liability of removing the wrong deceased or being accused of damaging the other cemetery.

Arranging for a removal becomes difficult when the motivation to do so is due to the abandonment of a cemetery. It may not only be impossible to authorize the removal, but access to accurate records of burial locations may not be possible. In a case such as this, contact the regulatory agency in your state that is responsible for cemeteries. It should be able to help you understand how to go about this as well as what you can and cannot do.

Typically, if a ground burial is removed, the cemetery will try to remove the vault with the casket in it. The vault is then moved to the new place of burial. If the vault is damaged, then the casket may need to be removed from it. If the removal is from a mausoleum crypt, the casket will be taken out of the crypt and transported using a special shipping container or air tray to the new place of burial. The condition of the casket will vary depending upon the length of time since the burial occurred, the material the casket is made of, and other conditions such as moisture in the ground. In some cases, it will be necessary to re-place the casket to facilitate the movement from one cemetery to another. 🍁

12. The End of Life

It's not easy for most people to talk about death. Nonetheless, as people face the end of life, there is often an increased desire to talk about it and plan for it. For most, the closer they are to that time and age, the more receptive and realistic they are about it. It's important not only to plan for what happens after death occurs but also to plan for what happens before death.

Death With Dignity

Many, if not most, experience a fear of dying. On a rational level, we know that the mortality rate is 100 percent per person. Nevertheless, coming to peace with our own mortality may be difficult emotionally. Elisabeth Kubler-Ross described the emotional states that often are experienced when facing a terminal illness as denial, anger, fear, depression, and acceptance. Although these feelings often are described as being in a sequence, it's important to understand that there isn't a "progression" through them. Most of the time the various emotions will come and go in a seemingly random pattern.

Denial is the "This can't be happening to me" response. Although we may have thought we might die one day, being told that it's imminent puts a new face on our thoughts about death. Consequently, it's common for people to believe that "The test results must be wrong" or "You've mixed up my tests with someone else."

As one begins to process the reality of pending death, they often experience anger—"Why is God doing this to me?" or "This isn't fair" or "I've too much to live for." The depth of the anger varies with the individuals but often is caused by a realization that one isn't in control of their own destiny.

When the anger begins to subside, it's often replaced with fear. Dying is an unknown. What the effect will be on the people you are close to is also scary. Most people are unsettled by ambiguity or unknown situations, and death is the ultimate unknown for many. Some find peace in their spiritual beliefs; others may not be in enough contact with their feelings to realize that they have fear.

Usually, the final stage is acceptance. This is an indication that the person has worked through the experience and come to a place of peace. In their own mind, they have accepted the inevitable.

Terminally ill people often are isolated, lonely, and powerless to control their surroundings. Thus it isn't surprising that as both the illness itself and the emotion of fear envelop them, often there is depression. The classical symptoms of depression are sleep problems, inability to concentrate, change in appetite, fatigue, and so on.

Dying people are grieving, too. It's common to have a need to say goodbye to everyone they know. This puts them through the experience of multiple anticipatory losses.

It's important to understand what terminally ill people may be going through, especially when someone you care about is in that position. Understanding the various emotions that they may experience can help you be more supportive. The emotions may be very intense and will reflect their own struggle. Although the words and actions may make it seem a personal affront to a friend or relative, understanding how the feelings may come out may help you temper your reactions and be more supportive.

Not only will the terminally ill person go through these emotions, it's quite likely that those close to them also will experience some of the same feelings.

All of us want to die with dignity. Many express a fear of becoming a "vegetable." They form a mental image of being unable to communicate and being held captive in a hospital bed with tubes, wires, breathing apparatus, and whatever else connected to them for a long period of time. Most of us don't like the thought of an end like that but, at the same time, don't want to have the medical equipment turned off when there is a chance of recovery. The problem is that there may be times when we cannot make decisions for ourselves or are unable to communicate our desires. The solution for this is a Durable Power of Attorney for Health Care. As mentioned before in Chapter 11, this legal document allows another person to make medical decisions for you in the event you are unable to make or communicate those decisions for yourself. In some states, standard forms are available from doctors or hospitals. Generally, the form gives you the opportunity to give some guidance about your wishes. This can be "don't resuscitate," "perform no heroic actions," or "keep me out of pain."

Hospice

A hospice is a place that is established to relieve the physical and emotional suffering of those who are dying. The origin of hospices stems from the Middle Ages, when places of charitable shelter offered rest and refreshment to pilgrims and travelers. Although hospitals for the terminally ill existed before the twentieth century, the modern hospice movement really developed following World War II.

Today, the hospice movement is dedicated to death with dignity. A hospice provides an empathetic, caring environment for those who are dying. The first priority is to address physical pain through medicine and physical therapies. However, a hospice generally will try to prevent pain rather than just treat it after it begins. The emotional side is met by support from loved ones and the hospice staff. Often this close bonding helps meet the emotional needs of family and friends, too.

Almost all hospice programs will facilitate a discussion about final arrangements, the Ceremony, burial, and cremation.

Usually, patients are admitted to a hospice by referral from a physician after determination that the patient has a short time to live—usually less than six months. However, you do not have to wait for your physician to bring up the subject. You should feel free to ask your physician about hospice care at anytime you think it might be appropriate for you or someone close to you. Hospice care can be provided in a health care facility, on an outpatient basis, or at home.

Here are three Internet sources for additional information about hospice care:

American Hospice Foundation, Washington D.C.
www.americanhospice.org

National Hospice Organization, Arlington, VA
www.nhpco.org

Hospice Net, Nashville, TN
www.hospicenet.org

13. Help & Resources

There are many possible sources of information and help. Increasingly, there is information about almost anything on the Internet, including access to public agencies, trade associations, special interest groups, mortuaries, and cemeteries. If you have questions regarding eligibility for government programs, most telephone books list contact information for government agencies. Appendix C also includes a number of possible resources that can be contacted for help or information.

The Role Of Government

Traditionally, the primary regulation of the cemetery and funeral professions has been at the state level. Although varying substantially from state to state, the areas of regulation include licensing, selling practices, required disclosures, various aspects of operations, and protection of trust funds. Local zoning laws govern where a cemetery or mortuary can be built. The federal government also has included mortuaries and cemeteries in most of its general business regulations. This includes mandatory "cooling off" periods for in-home sales and restrictions on telephone solicitations.

Federal Trade Commission Funeral Rule

In 1982, the Federal Trade Commission (FTC) adopted a Funeral Rule. The process of creating the rule was controversial as have been the two subsequent reviews of it. Overall, the intent is easy to comprehend: consumers have a right to accurate information about pricing, goods, and services. Here are the major items covered in the FTC Funeral Rule:

* General Price List.

* Representations about cash advance items.

* Representations about embalming.

* Representations about caskets.

Many funeral directors—led by the National Funeral Directors Association (NFDA)—fought the FTC Funeral Rule because they didn't like the idea of being required to disclose all their prices. Some funeral establishments, like Forest Lawn, didn't like the process or the rigid form of disclosure but saw only good in requiring all mortuaries to provide accurate price information. Forest Lawn had long done that. In fact, it had dropped out of the NFDA in the 1950s because it didn't agree with their position that price advertising was "unprofessional." For decades before the FTC Funeral Rule, Forest Lawn had run ads suggesting that consumers should "shop and compare." This may seem somewhat self-serving, but it is included here to underscore an institutional belief that consumers should be able to get full and accurate information to use in decision-making. Many in the funeral profession were disclosing this information long before the existence of the FTC Funeral Rule.

The portion dealing with cash advance items prohibits a firm from labeling an item as a cash advance if there is any profit or overhead in it. An example of a common cash advance item would be a clergy honorarium. As long as a mortuary does not call an item a cash advance, it can set whatever price it wants.

The FTC Funeral Rule prohibits representing that embalming is required. Similarly, a mortuary may not require that a casket be used for cremation. However, the mortuary may determine what type of alterative container(s) it sells.

The FTC has been criticized for lax enforcement of the Funeral Rule. That may be a fair assessment, but the real issue for any consumer is whether or not any firm you are doing business with is willing to tell you what its prices are and to discuss honestly and openly all questions you have about pricing and arrangements. Why would you want to deal with anyone who doesn't want to treat you like a capable, informed, adult decision-maker?

The reality is that, over time, consumers have become more sophisticated about purchases they make. Most mortuaries understand this and are more than willing to openly discuss pricing and services.

State Regulatory Agencies

Other than the FTC Funeral Rule and general federal consumer law, the mortuary and cemetery professions are regulated at the state level. Not surprisingly, each state has a different view of what sort of regulations are appropriate for the two professions. Many states have either phone hot lines or web sites to provide information to consumers. Also, phone books in larger cities often include a listing of government agencies. Although a state regulatory agency will try to be helpful, most cannot help with problems that fall outside of their regulatory authority.

If Things Go Wrong

There are times when things go wrong in connection with a Ceremony, burial, or cremation. Problems can be caused by errors made by the mortuary, cemetery, or crematory; external factors like weather; disagreements within families; or even by incorrect or conflicting information being provided by families.

Although it's not always easy, it's important to realize that when a death occurs it is a very stressful time. Sometimes there is a lot of anger over the death and there is no one to vent it on. Then there is an error of some sort and it gets blown out of proportion. I don't say this because I don't think firms make errors—they depend upon human beings and, much as they try to avoid errors, mistakes will be made. Rather, it's important to understand your own emotional state when there is a problem. If you want to get a specific outcome for correction of the problem, it may be a time to do the proverbial "count to ten before acting" rather than just blowing up. On the other hand, yelling can be cathartic.

Sometimes, too, the mortuary, cemetery, or crematory is caught in the middle. For example, if half the surviving children want cremation of a parent and the other half are adamantly opposed, the funeral director probably will try to mediate. If that is unsuccessful, they will have little choice but to suggest that a court order resolving the dispute should be obtained. Or suppose that two women claim to be the only wife of a deceased (yes, it does happen). The mortuary is in a position where it can't really believe either one!

Appendix C lists a number of organizations that can be helpful. Some of the trade associations have staff members who are specifically assigned the task of helping consumers resolve problems with members.

Where To Start

The place to start when you have a complaint or problem is usually with the company you have been dealing with. Most mortuaries, cemeteries, and crematories view themselves as being in the business of providing service and want to do things right. Therefore, they do want to try to correct problems. Depending on the culture of the organization you are dealing with, you may need to ask to speak to a supervisor or manager when you have a problem with an employee. Don't hesitate to do that if you feel you aren't getting anywhere.

Do bring up the error as soon as you find out about it. There are several reasons for this. First, the sooner you do, the sooner the error can be addressed. Second, you can put the problem on someone else's shoulders to solve rather than bearing it yourself. Third, you have more credibility. When someone waits sixty days to bring up an error, the person receiving the complaint is apt to believe that it wasn't very important to you if you waited that long. This is particularly true when it has not only been a long time, but the first payment is now due. In that case, it looks like the complaining party is trying to dodge a bill rather than actually having a valid complaint!

Expect the solution to fit the size of the problem. Living and working in litigation-prone California, I realize that many view the legal system as a lottery.

Financial

A number of government programs are affected by a death—Social Security for Supplemental Security Income and veterans benefits being the most common.

Social Security

Under the Social Security system, some survivors of workers are eligible for a lump-sum death benefit. These include:

* A widow or widower sixty or over—or any age if caring for a qualified child.

* A divorced widow age sixty or older if the marriage lasted at least ten years.

* Unmarried children up to age eighteen

As rules change with time, it's best to contact the Social Security Administration to determine eligibility. Look under "U.S. Government" in the phone book for a local office or call (800) 772-1213.

When contacting the Social Security Administration, having the following will help:

* Deceased's social security number.

* Applicant's social security number.

✶ Proof of worker's death.

✶ Proof of marriage if applicant is applying for widow's or widower's benefits.

✶ Birth certificates of children if they are to receive benefits.

✶ For the most recent tax year, the Form W-2 for the deceased worker or federal tax return if self-employed.

✶ Proof of support if applicant is applying for benefits as a dependent parent or grandchild of the deceased worker.

The mortuary is required to notify the Social Security Administration of the death, but the family must file for any benefits.

Supplemental Security Income (SSI)

To become eligible for Supplemental Security Income limits are placed on the assets that can be held. For individuals this is currently $2,000 and for a couple $3,000. These limits also apply to maintaining eligibility.

Under most circumstances, funds set aside in a prearrangement fund for a "burial fund" and "cemetery space" are not included in determining eligibility. There are limitations on the amounts that may be set aside for this, unless the funds are set aside in an irrevocable manner. Setting aside funds irrevocably means that the beneficiary or person receiving benefits can no longer control or have access to the asset or cash.

Contact the Social Security Administration for more information on this program.

Veterans Benefits

Most members of the U.S. Armed Forces who died on active duty and veterans whose discharge from military service was not dishonorable are eligible for burial in national cemeteries. There are further limitations to this that began in 1980.

Burial in a national cemetery is also available to the spouse, widow, or widower of any eligible veteran who has not remarried. A veteran's dependent minor children are also eligible.

The rules for eligibility for burial benefits and plot allowances vary according to when death occurred and the reason for discharge or retirement from the service. Plot allowances are not given to veterans buried in a national cemetery.

Veterans eligible for burial in a national cemetery and who are buried after 1978 are entitled to a government-provided memorial whether or not they are buried in a national cemetery. The memorial can be of bronze or granite. As noted earlier, each cemetery, including those operated by the Veterans Administration, sets its own regulations about what types of memorials it will allow. Just as with private cemeteries, if a burial is to take place in a national cemetery, you should check with the specific cemetery to learn what its requirements are.

Public Aid Funerals

Local government has the responsibility of taking care of those who die without the means to cover their own burial expenses. Depending upon jurisdiction, this may be a city, county, or other agency. While historically this was done in so-called potter's fields, many urban areas now cremate the indigent and then bury the cremated remains in common graves. 🍁

Appendix A. Your Information

There are many records that are important during life as well as when death occurs. Often finding these, though, can be a challenge for those left behind. Here are some thoughts about what information and paperwork might be needed.

In addition to the "business" records that are important, leaving thoughts about your life can be very meaningful. Also, thinking about the thoughts you'd like to leave can help you with the process of deciding how you want to say goodbye.

Financial Records and Valuable Papers (what they are; where they are kept)

Bank accounts

Insurance policies (life, homeowners, and so on)

Loans, mortgages, and credit cards

Brokerage and investment accounts

Retirement plans

Real estate deeds

Vehicle and boat title documents

Birth certificates

Marriage certificates or licenses

Will

Deed to cemetery property

Military discharge papers

Tax records

Safe deposit box locations

Trust documents

Information about other assets & liabilities

Personal Information

Family history

People to contact (names and phone number or other contact information): relatives, close friends, executor, doctor, and attorney

People that have had the greatest effect on my life

People you'd like to say goodbye to

My fondest memories (and where are the photos, scrapbooks, & diaries)

Things I'd like to be remembered for

What you are most proud of

Things you wish you had said

Things you wish you had done

If you could live life over again, what would you spend less time on? More time on?

Your favorite quote

About My Ceremony

Who to call

What the Ceremony should be like

Where the Ceremony should be held

Cemetery property

Appendix B. Goods And Services

Making price comparisons between competing mortuaries is particularly difficult. For those who wish to try this, the following is a list of goods and services that you may encounter. With the trend toward package pricing, it's especially important to understand what is included or not included. Use the list below to help compare what is included, or not included, in a given mortuary's offering. Although the list is divided into categories, they are not meant to imply that you must go to a certain type of provider—mortuary, cemetery, crematory, or retail casket store—to purchase the item. For example, outer burial containers are often sold by mortuaries, cemeteries, and retail casket stores.

Mortuary Services

Minimum Undertaking or Basic Services (also known as the "non-declinable fee")

Care and Preparation (includes personnel, use of equipment and mortuary facility for dressing, cosmetics, and hair styling)

Visitation (viewing)

Preservative Refrigeration

Funeral Ceremony

Vigil or Prayer Service

Memorial Service

Graveside or Nicheside Ceremony

Limousine with Driver

Casket Coach (hearse)

Flower Car or Van

Receiving Deceased from Another Mortuary

Forwarding Deceased to Another Mortuary

Music (soloist, organist, or other musician)

Funeral Goods

Memorial Register Book

Memory Folders (service programs)

Acknowledgement Cards

Caskets

Shipping Container

Alternative Cremation Container (cardboard box or pressed wood container for handling deceased in a no-service cremation situation)

Flowers (may be casket sprays, plants, standing arrangements, or other)

Cemetery Services

Cemetery Property

Burial (also known as "interment fee" or "opening and closing")

Memorial Installation

Cemetery Goods

Cremated Remains Container (urn or other container)

Outer Burial Container

Memorials (monument, marker, tombstone)

Flower Vases

Miscellaneous

Extra Charges for Weekend or Late Services

Endowment Care Fund Deposit

Appendix C. For More Information

Information sources listed are from *Funerals: A Consumer Guide* by the Federal Trade Commission (June 2000).

Most states have a licensing board that regulates the funeral profession. You may contact the board in your state for information or help. If you want additional information about making final arrangements and the options available, you may want to contact interested business, professional, and consumer groups. Some of the biggest are:

AARP Fulfillment

601 E Street, NW
Washington, DC 20049
1-800-424-3410
www.aarp.org

AARP is a nonprofit, nonpartisan organization dedicated to helping older Americans achieve lives of independence, dignity, and purpose. Its publications, "Funeral Goods and Services" and "Pre-Paying for Your Funeral," are available free by writing to the above address. This and other funeral-related information is posted on the AARP website.

Council of Better Business Bureaus, Inc.

4200 Wilson Blvd., Suite 800
Arlington, VA 22203-1838
www.bbb.org/library/funeral.asp

Better Business Bureaus are private, nonprofit organizations that promote ethical business standards and voluntary self-regulation of business practices. The BBB's website offers information about prearrangement.

Funeral Consumers Alliance

PO Box 10
Hinesburg, VT 05461
1-800-458-5563
www.funerals.org

FCA, a nonprofit, educational organization that supports increased funeral consumer protection, is affiliated with the Funeral and Memorial Society of America (FAMSA).

Cremation Association of North America

401 North Michigan Avenue
Chicago, IL 60611
(312) 321-6806
www.cremationassociation.org

CANA is an association of crematories, cemeteries, and mortuaries that offer cremation.

International Cemetery and Funeral Association

1895 Preston White Drive, Suite 220
Reston, VA 20191
1-800-645-7700
www.icfa.org

ICFA is a nonprofit association of cemeteries, mortuaries, crematories, and monument retailers that offers informal mediation of consumer complaints through its Cemetery

Consumer Service Council. Its website provides information and advice under "Consumer Resources."

International Order of the Golden Rule

13523 Lakefront Drive
St. Louis, MO 63045
1-800-637-8030
www.ogr.org

OGR is an international association of about 1,300 independent mortuaries.

Jewish Funeral Directors of America

Seaport Landing
150 Lynnway, Suite 506
Lynn, MA 01902
(781) 477-9300
www.jfda.org

JFDA is an international association of mortuaries serving the Jewish community.

National Funeral Directors Association

13625 Bishop's Drive
Brookfield, WI 53005
1-800-228-6332
www.nfda.org/resources

NFDA is the largest professional association of funeral directors.

National Funeral Directors and Morticians Association

3951 Snapfinger Parkway, Suite 570
Decatur, GA 30035
1-800-434-0958
www.nfdma.com

NFDMA is a national association primarily of African-American mortuaries.

Selected Independent Funeral Homes
(formerly National Selected Morticians)

5 Revere Drive, Suite 340
Northbrook, IL 60062-8009
1-800-323-4219
www.nsm.org

NSM is a national association of funeral firms that have agreed to comply with its Code of Good Funeral Practice. Consumers may request a variety of publications through NSM's affiliate, the Consumer Information Bureau, Inc.

Funeral Service Consumer Assistance Program

PO Box 486
Elm Grove, WI 53122-0486
1-800-662-7666

FSCAP is a nonprofit consumer service designed to help people understand funeral service and related topics and to help them resolve funeral service concerns. FSCAP service representatives and an intervener assist consumers in identifying needs, addressing complaints, and resolving problems. Free brochures on funeral related topics are available.

Funeral Service Educational Foundation

13625 Bishop's Drive
Brookfield, WI 53005
1-877-402-5900

FSEF is a nonprofit foundation dedicated to advancing professionalism in funeral service and to enhancing public knowledge and understanding through education and research.

Federal Trade Commission

You can file a complaint with the FTC by contacting the Consumer Response Center by phone, toll-free, at 1-877-FTC-HELP (382-4357); TDD: 202-326-2502; by mail: Consumer Response Center, Federal Trade Commission, 600 Pennsylvania Avenue, NW, Washington, DC 20580; or on the Internet at www.ftc.gov, using the online complaint form. Although the Commission cannot resolve individual problems for consumers, it can act against a company if it sees a pattern of possible law violations.

Notes:

Chapter 2

[1] Theresa Rando, p. 267.

Chapter 3

[1] Even when there isn't a statutory prohibition, most cemeteries have regulations that limit burial to human remains.

Chapter 5

[1] Ron Russell, "Unholy Alliance," www.newtimesla.com (Originally published by New Times L.A. Dec 27, 2001)

[2] Rev. Mike Macdonald, "Commentary: Wedding, funeral music should glorify God," United Methodist News Service, June 12, 2002, umns.umc.org/01/sep/371.htm.

[3] Rando, p. 266.

Chapter 6

[1] Wirthlin Group.

[2] Wirthlin Worldwide, p. 5.

[3] Title 40, Code of Federal Regulations, Chapter 1, Part 229, § 229.1 Burial at sea.

[4] California Health & Safety Code § 7054.7(b).

[5] UPS United States, "Terms and Conditions of Service: for customers located in the 48 contiguous states," Oct. 15, 2003, www.ups.com/content/us/en/resources/service/terms/service.html.

[6] FedEx, "FedEx Express Terms and Conditions: Shipping items prohibited," FedEx, Oct. 15, 2003, www.fedex.com/us/services/express/termsandconditions/us/prohibiteditems.html.

Chapter 7

[1] For example, California Health & Safety Code § 7100.1 says, in part, that "prior to death [a person] may...specify funeral goods and services to be provided. Unless there is a statement to the contrary that is signed

and dated by the decedent, the direction may not be altered, changed, or otherwise amended in any material way."

Chapter 8

[1] The terms cancellation and revocation may have different meanings under contract law. For ease of presentation, only the term cancellation is used here.

Chapter 9

[1] This restriction is primarily to keep cemetery/mortuary combinations out of the state. Small funeral directors have historically fought competition from combinations by promoting restrictive licensing laws. Usually, the result of less competition is fewer choices for consumers and higher prices.

[2] National Funeral Directors Association, "NFDA Fact Sheets," www.nfda.org/nfdafactsheets.php, July 16, 2003.

[3] A 5 percent income rate is probably high for a fund that is invested in some mix of stocks and bonds that will enable it to get some level of capital appreciation to offset the long-term effects of inflation. State laws vary substantially about what these funds may be invested in.

[4] Ultimately, the Department of Consumers Affairs got its wish. The California Cemetery Board and the Board of Funeral Directors and Embalmers, both of which had a majority of public, non-industry members, were eliminated and the regulation of cemeteries, crematories, and mortuaries was turned over to a new Cemetery and Funeral Bureau within the Department.

[5] Some states do not allow cemeteries to sell memorials. In most states memorials can be purchased from cemeteries, mortuaries, monument dealers, or casket stores.

[6] "Basic services" is a term from the Federal Trade Commission's Funeral Rule. Sometimes, it is referred to as a "non-declinable fee."

Chapter 10

[1] See the section on the FTC Funeral Rule in Chapter Twelve for a discussion of the non-declinable fee mortuaries may charge.

[2] The "usually" qualifier is because some cemeteries have mausoleums with lower floors that are below ground level.

Glossary

Although many terms used by cemeteries and mortuaries have industry-wide meaning, some terms mean different things in different parts of the country or even to competing organizations. This glossary is presented as an aid to consumers in understanding terms that may be used in dealing with cemeteries or mortuaries. Throughout the body of this book, an attempt was made to use the more common terms that an average consumer might use. Hopefully, this made the text more understandable, but it also may have been less than precise. The definitions and terms contained in this glossary are intended to be more precise, while providing cross-references to more common terms. If you have any questions when someone uses a term, don't hesitate to ask—consumer-oriented organizations are always willing to explain their services and merchandise.

alternative container A non metal receptacle without ornamentation or interior lining that is designed to hold human remains and is made of cardboard, pressed wood, composition materials (with or without an outside covering), or pouches of canvas or other materials.

ashes *See* cremated remains.

at need At time of death, including immediately following or when impending.

before need *See* preneed.

below ground crypt *See* lawn crypt.

burial *See* entombment and interment. syn. inhumation.

burial permit A legal document issued by a local authority authorizing final disposition of human remains.

cash advance Any item of service or merchandise described to a purchaser as a "cash advance," "accommodation," "cash disbursement," or similar term. A cash advance item is also any item obtained from a third party and paid for by the seller on the purchaser's behalf.

Cash advance items may include, but are not limited to, cemetery or crematory services, pallbearers, public transportation, clergy honoraria, flowers, musicians or singers, obituary notices, gratuities, and death certificates.

casket A rigid container for the interment of human remains. May be made of wood, metal, or like material and are ornamented and lined with fabric. Wooden models include cloth covered soft woods and hardwoods finished like fine furniture. Metal caskets are most commonly made of steel, copper, or bronze. Additionally, metal caskets may be "protective" or "sealing" because they have a gasket around the lid. The FTC Funeral Trade Rule and some states have specific requirements regarding representations about sealing caskets.

cemetery (1) A place dedicated to and used, or intended to be used, for the final disposition and memorialization of human remains. (2) A place for burial of dead human remains.

cemetery authority A person, partnership, or corporation that owns or controls a cemetery or conducts cemetery business.

cenotaph A memorial in honor of a deceased person who is interred elsewhere.

coffin A container for burial of human remains, usually applied to a hexagonal shaped container. *Also see* casket.

columbarium *pl.* -ia, iums A structure, room, or space in a building or structure used, or intended to be used, for the placement of cremated remains.

cremated remains The bone fragments remaining after the cremation process that may include the residue of any foreign materials that were cremated with the human remains. After removal of metallic parts of caskets and prosthetics, cremated remains are usually processed by crushing or grinding to achieve a uniform consistency.

cremated remains container A receptacle in which cremated remains are placed after cremation.

cremation The irreversible process of reducing human remains to bone fragments through intense heat and evaporation in a specifically designed furnace or retort that may include any other mechanical or thermal process, whereby the bone fragments are pulverized or otherwise further reduced in size or volume. Cremation is a process and is not final disposition. (Note: some states don't agree with this and maintain that cremation itself is a form of disposition.)

cremation container An enclosed receptacle that is combustible, rigid, and leak-resistant and is designed to hold human remains prior to cremation; includes non-metallic caskets.

crematory A structure containing a furnace or retort used or intended to be used for the cremation of human remains.

crypt A concrete enclosure for interment. Mausoleum crypts are generally above ground and in buildings. Crypts in garden mausoleums also are usually above ground but are open to the outside rather than being in an enclosed building. Crypts also may be installed in large groups underground in lawn sections—See lawn crypt. Lawn crypts do not require the use of an additional outer burial container. Lawn crypts are sometimes referred to as garden crypts.

death certificate A legal document containing vital statistics pertaining to the life and death of the deceased. Must be accepted and filed with the proper agency before a burial permit is issued.

deed A document conveying a right of interment in specific cemetery property. Usually doesn't convey any fee ownership.

direct cremation Disposition of human remains by cremation without formal viewing, visitation, or ceremony with the body present.

direct disposition Any final disposition of human remains without formal viewing, visitation, or ceremony with the body present.

disinterment Removing human remains that have been interred. *Also see* interment.

embalmer A person authorized by law to engage in embalming.

embalming A procedure where human remains are chemically treated by injection and/or topical application for temporary preservation, including, but not limited to, the act of disinfecting, preserving, and restoring the human remains to a natural life-like appearance. The preservation is intended to allow for adequate time to plan a funeral service and for friends and family to travel from out-of-town, rather than for any long-term protection from decomposition.

endowment care The maintenance, repair, and care of all places in the cemetery, subject to the rules and regulations of the cemetery authority. May also be known as endowed care, perpetual care, improvement care, permanent care, maintenance fund, and so on.

endowment care fund An irrevocable trust fund set aside by law with a trustee, where the earnings from the trust principal provide for the long-term care of the cemetery. In some states referred to as a "Perpetual Care Fund."

entombment The act of placing human remains in a crypt.

final disposition The lawful disposal of human remains whether by interment, burial at sea, scattering, and so on.

FTC Funeral Trade Rule In 1982, the Federal Trade Commission promulgated a set of regulations requiring disclosure of price and other information by mortuaries and other sellers of funeral services and merchandise.

funeral director A person who manages a mortuary. In many states, this person is also an embalmer. This definition varies according to individual state laws and regulations.

funeral The ceremony held to commemorate the deceased with the remains present.

funeral establishment *See* mortuary.

funeral home *See* mortuary.

garden crypt *See* lawn crypt.

garden mausoleum An outdoor mausoleum. Sometimes called "wall crypts" because of the configuration of the crypts and to avoid confusion with indoor mausoleums. *Also see* mausoleum.

grave space A space of ground in a cemetery that is used or intended to be used for ground burial.

guaranteed price prepaid contract A contract with a fixed price for services or merchandise purchased before death. *Also see* non-guaranteed price prepaid contract.

immediate burial Disposition of human remains by burial without formal viewing, visitation, or ceremony with the body present, except for a graveside service.

interment (1) Final disposition by burial in ground, entombment in a mausoleum, or placement of cremated remains in a niche. (2) The process of making an interment, including all administrative, clerical, legal, and mechanical services performed by the cemetery authority in conjunction with the opening of an interment space and closing of the interment space after the remains have been placed in the space.

interment right The right to inter human remains in a particular interment space in the cemetery.

interment right owner The person or persons who lawfully possess an interment right. There is a presumption of ownership in favor of the person listed as the owner in the records of the cemetery. *syn.* property owner.

interment space A space intended for the final disposition of human remains, including, but not limited to, a grave space, mausoleum crypt, garden crypt, columbarium, and lawn crypt.

inurnment The act of putting cremated remains in an urn.

lawn crypt A pre-installed enclosed chamber, usually constructed of reinforced concrete, poured in place or precast units installed in quantity, either side by side or multiple depth, and covered by earth or sod. Also may be known as a garden crypt (not the above ground type), below ground crypt, or turf-top crypt.

marker *See* memorial.

mausoleum *pl.* -leums, -lea. A chamber or structure used, or intended to be used, for entombment. A building that houses crypts for burial. A community mausoleum is for many families, and a private mausoleum is generally sold for the use of a single family. Some vendors sell what they call private or family mausoleums with only a few spaces. Many of these are more correctly called sarcophagi.

memorial The physical identification of an interment space. Generally has at least the name, date of birth, and date of death of the deceased and may include an epitaph or commemoration of the life, deeds, or career of the deceased person. These may be in the form of bronze or granite tablets flush with the ground, upright monuments, individual cut out bronze letters applied to the front of a mausoleum crypt, statuary, benches, or other artwork or architectural features. Other terms that might be used are memorial tablet (flush bronze memorial), marker, headstone, crypt plate, or garden plaque. *Also see* cenotaph.

memorialization The existence of a memorial or the process of erecting a memorial.

memorial-park A cemetery which has adopted a park[-]like style and abolished the use of upright memorials. As envisioned by Dr. Hubert Eaton who coined the term, a memorial-park has "sweeping lawns" and also must be inspirational, "...a place that uplifts and educates a community." Some cemeteries continue to allow upright memorials but call themselves memorial-parks because they have some sections where upright memorials are not allowed.

memorial service A ceremony commemorating the deceased without the remains present.

memorial society A membership organization that distributes information about funerals. May promote methods of prearrangement, changes to funeral laws, and offer referrals to specific funeral homes. Generally not regulated.

monument An upright memorial, including what used to be called a tombstone. Also includes large structures like obelisks, usually made from granite.

mortuary A place of business used in the care, planning, and preparation for final disposition or transportation of human remains. Operations may include arranging and conducting funerals, sales of services and funeral merchandise, and embalming.

niche A space within a columbarium used, or intended to be used, for inurnment of cremated remains.

opening and closing *See* interment.

outer burial container A container that is designed for placement in the grave space around the casket, including, but not limited to, containers commonly known as burial vaults, grave boxes, and grave liners.

perpetual care Generally replaced by the term "endowment care." *See* endowment care.

potter's fields A cemetery for paupers. The term comes from Matthew 27:7 when the chief priests determined what to do with the thirty pieces of silver returned by Judas: "So they took counsel, and bought with them the potter's field, to bury strangers in."

predeveloped Designated areas or buildings within a cemetery that have been mapped and planned for future construction but are not yet completed.

prearrangement Specifying future cemetery or funeral commodities or services and funding a method of paying for the future purchase. Purchase may be done by a single payment or installment payments. Most common is making financial provision for future purchase without current purchase of goods or services. Not necessarily a price guaran-tee but often perceived to include one.

prefinancing *See* prearrangement.

preneed Prior to death or prior to an impending death. Not at need.

prepaid purchase *See* prearrangement.

preplanning Making and recording the preneed decisions for inter-ment or funeral services.

private mausoleum A mausoleum for one family. *See* mausoleum and sarcophagus.

processing cremated remains The grinding or pulverizing of the bone fragments remaining from a cremation to achieve a more uniform consistency. *Also see* cremation.

property owner *See* interment right holder.

residue Cremated remains that are imbedded in cracks and uneven spaces of the cremation chamber or in the cremated remains con-tainer and cannot be removed through reasonable manual contact with sweeping or scraping equipment.

rules and regulations Rules adopted by a cemetery to govern uses, care, control, and management as well as other restrictions deemed necessary by the governing board for protection of the cemetery.

sarcophagus *pl.* -gi. A structure of marble or stone, or covered with marble or stone, for entombment of one or more casketed human remains. May be indoors.

special care Any care provided, or to be provided, in excess of endow-ment care in accordance with the specific directions of any donor of funds for such purposes. Funds for special care may be held in a trust fund similar to an endowment care fund.

tombstone *See* monument.

traditional cemetery A cemetery that allows or requires traditional upright memorials. *See* memorial-park.

undertaker *See* funeral director.

urn A receptacle for cremated remains. Should not be confused with an alternative container or cremation container.

vault *See* outer burial container.

wall crypt *See* garden mausoleum.

Bibliography

Bates, Bill K., "Why Personalize? The Value of Human Relations in Funeral Service," *The Independent*, May/June 2000.

Becker, Ernest, *The Denial of Death*, New York: Free Press Paperbacks, 1997.

Bennett, Amanda and Terence B. Foley, *In Memoriam: A practical guide to planning a memorial service*, New York: Fireside, 1997.

Carey, Benedict, "When a 'Good Death' Isn't for Everyone," *The Los Angeles Times*, August 20, 2001, sec. S, p. 1.

Carlson, Lisa, *Caring for the Dead: Your final act of love*, Hinesburg, Vermont: Upper Access, Inc., 1998.

Correa, Barbara, "Investing for Eternity," *Daily News*, Sunday Business section, June 1, 2003, p. 1.

Cox, Meg, "Into the Winds of the Great Beyond," *Worth*, July/August 2001.

Cullen, Lisa Takeuchi, "What a Way to Go," *Time*, July 7, 2003.

Eskin, Sandra B., "Preneed Funeral and Burial Agreements: A summary of state statutes," AARP, 1999.

"Final Arrangements," *Consumer Reports*, May 2001, pp. 28-33.

"GAO Report to Congressional Requesters, 'Death Care Industry: Regulation varies across states and by industry segment'" (GAO-03-757), United States General Accounting Office, 2003.

Goralski, Margaret A., Ellen Rusconi-Black, and Robert B. Bailey, *Death...A Practical Guide to the Choices that Lie Beyond!*, San Jose: Writers Club Press, 2000.

Hamilton, Denise, "Putting Your Wishes in Writing," *The Los Angeles Times*, August 20, 2001, sec. S, p. 1.

Irion, Paul E., *The Funeral: Vestige or value?*, Nashville: Abingdon Press, 1966.

————*The Funeral and the Mourners: Pastoral care of the bereaved*, Nashville: Abington Press,1954.

Kubler-Ross, M.D., Elizabeth, *On Death and Dying*, New York: Simon & Schuster, 1969.

Laderman, Gary, *Rest In Peace: A cultural history of death and the funeral home in twentieth-century America*, New York: Oxford University Press, 2003.

Lagorce, Adue, "Personalizing Your Final Resting Place," *Forbes.com*, October 29, 2003.

Llewellyn, John F., *A Cemetery Should Be Forever: The challenge to managers and directors*, Glendale, California: Tropico Press, 1999.

Marsa, Linda, "Last Days Needn't Be Spent in Agony," *The Los Angeles Times*, August 20, 2001, sec. S, p. 1.

Means to a Better End: A report on dying in America Today, Washington, D.C.: Last Acts, November 2000.

Mims, Cederic, *When We Die: The science, culture, and rituals of death*, New York: St. Martin's Griffin, 1998.

Nuland, Sherwin B., *How We Die: Reflections on life's final chapter*, New York: Alfred A. Knopf, 1994.

Prothero, Stephen, *Purified by Fire: A history of cremation in America*, Berkley: University of California Press, 2001.

————"Sifting the Ashes," *The Wall Street Journal* (On-Line Edition), April 27, 2001.

Rando, Theresa A., *How to Go on Living When Someone You Love Dies*, New York: Bantam Books, 1991.

Romain, Trevor, *What on Earth Do You Do When Someone Dies?*, Minneapolis: Free Spirit Publishing Inc., 1999.

Schiff, Harriet Sarnoff, *Living Through Mourning: Finding comfort and hope when a loved one has died*, New York: Penguin Books, 1987.

Sittser, Gerald L., *A Grace Disguised: How the soul grows through loss*, Grand Rapids, Michigan: Zondervan Publishing House, 1996.

Siwolop, Sana, "The Perils of Planning One's Own Prepaid Funeral," *New York Times*, August 21, 2001.

Sublette, Kathleen and Martin Flagg, *Final Celebrations: A guide for personal and family funeral planning*, Ventura: Pathfinder Publishing of California 1992.

Tatelbaum, Judy, *The Courage to Grieve*, New York: Harper & Row, 1984.

Wakin, Daniel J., "Archbishop of Newark Bans Eulogies at Funeral Masses," *The New York Times*, January 23, 2003, Late Edition – Final, sec. B, p. 5.

Welshons, John, *Awakening From Grief: Finding the road back to joy*, Little Falls, New Jersey: Open Heart Publications, 2000.

Wirthlin Group, 1995, "Study of American Attitudes Toward Ritualization and Memorialization," September 1995.

Wirthlin Worldwide, "Executive Summary of the Funeral and Memorialization Counsel Study of American Attitudes Toward Ritualization and Memorialization: 1999 Update," 2000.

Zaslow, Jeffrey, "Moving On: '...And John Was a Terrible Gambler': When Eulogists Get Carried Away," *The Wall Street Journal*, July 10, 2003, sec. D, p. 1.

Index

About the Author

John Llewellyn has spent more than three decades in the cemetery and funeral industries. Since 1988, he has been president and chief executive officer of Forest Lawn Memorial-Parks and Mortuaries in Southern California. He has been president of the International Cemetery and Funeral Association and the Interment Association of California as well as being an officer and director of the California Mortuary Alliance and the Western Cemetery Alliance. Active in the community, John has served as a hospital, university, and foundation trustee as well as a director of more than two dozen non-profit organizations including serving as chairman of the Braille Institute of America, Los Angeles Area Council-Boy Scouts of America, and the Employers Group.

A previous book, *A Cemetery Should Be Forever: The challenge to officers and directors*, was widely acclaimed by members of the cemetery industry in the United States and Europe as capturing the complexities of managing a cemetery and a clear statement of the importance of those responsible for cemeteries having a long-range view of the needs of the cemetery.

John graduated from the University of Redlands with a major in economics and received an MBA from the University of Southern California. He lives in Pasadena, California, with his two dogs.